To max
Protour
for your
a expertise!

MW01223971

Dear Lucy

A Memoir

Phyllis Martin

Glue Pot Press

New Orleans, Louisiana

DEAR LUCY A MEMOIR

Copyright © 2020 Phyllis Martin

All rights reserved.

ISBN: 978-0-9898392-9-7

Designed and published by Max Marbles at the Glue Pot Press in
New Orleans, Louisiana
editor@gluepotpress.com

Manufactured in the United States of America

First Printing in May of 2020

For Ron who convinced me to follow my dreams

and

For Steve who walks beside me as I pursue those dreams

CONTENTS

Dear Lucy,

I wanted to write a book for you before you embark on your life outside the safety of your home, out from the loving wings of your parents. This book is about my life, why things are as they are and how I have navigated and sometimes been swept along the path of my journey. I know you have already begun the process, just as a fledgling robin slowly emerges from her egg, tentatively testing the nest floor, wobbly at first, but stronger and steady until that first test of her wings.

Can she fly?

Will she fly?

She must fly.

You have been blessed with parents who created a nurturing safe world where independent thinking, creativity and conviction for social justice was modeled and encouraged. Gender equality was and continues to be, an overtly supported value and assumption.

I envy you for that.

FORWARD

HUMAN DEVELOPMENT: NATURE AND NURTURE

What makes a person become who they are?

The nature versus nurture debate argues whether human behavior is determined by the environment, either prenatal or during a person's life, or by a person's genetics.

Behaviorists propose that a baby is born as a "tabula rasa", or "blank slate"; whatever and whoever they become is a result of exposure to stimuli. In simple terms, a child becomes who they are as a result of the behavioral reinforcements, including the quality of parenting, present in their world. Behaviorism dominated the psychological approach to human development in the 1950's and 1960's and B.F. Skinner popularized the theory that all behavior stems from one's environment.

Fortunately, human development is a bit more complicated than behaviorism would suggest. From the 1970's to the end of the 20th century, a noticeable shift occurred as knowledge of the brain and genetics began to promote the appreciation of nature as a critical influence on a person's thoughts, feelings, and behavior. Twin studies eventually became easier to perform and by the late 1990's an overwhelming amount of evidence had accumulated that amounted to a refutation of extreme behaviorism.

We are all born with a genetic template which informs our emotional, mental, and physical characteristics. The environment into which we are born then molds and shapes the formation of that genetic predisposition.

We are who we are because we are

Phyllis Martin, Psy.D.
Clinical Psychologist

.

PROLOGUE

MY STORY BEGINS

I thought I was going to drown. My husband Ron and I were attending a family campout with our twelve-year-old daughter Beth and she her two cousins had floated on an inner tube into the middle of the lake. I stood on the beach watching them as dark storm clouds loomed over-head and, since we had no boat, I decided that I would swim out to rescue them. I thought of myself as a good swimmer. However, except for an occasional dip in a hot tub and a few laps in a motel swimming pool, I had not really gone swimming for about twenty years. So there I was, half-way between the shore and the girls. I was exhausted, out of breath and felt like a limp noodle. I did what we have all heard we should do in such circumstances. I tried floating on my back to rest. It was not, however, restful or helpful in any way. I gazed at the black abyss beneath me. I couldn't swim any further.

I'd like to say that I started praying and that Jesus Himself appeared in that moment of crisis and that I miraculously resumed swimming with new vigor and stamina. But no. I didn't pray. The only thought I had was "Shit. I'm going to drown, and Ron is going to have to tell Mom that her daughter is dead." I began swimming again. One stroke. One stroke. One stroke. Focus..... One stroke. As I closed in on the girls, Leanne, the youngest, noticed me and laughed "It's Auntie Phyl! Let's get away so she can't reach us!".

I yelled for them to stop but my voice was weak. I kept swimming. One stroke. One stroke. Focus on one stroke. One stroke at a time. After what seemed like at least a million strokes, I reached the girls and grabbed onto the inner tube, gasping for breath. I held on as we paddled back to shore. We shivered together in the cool breeze on the beach as the sky became dark. The clouds finally broke open and rain pounded out little bubbles on the sandy beach as the wind swept away empty soda cans.

That evening we sat around the campfire singing, telling jokes, and eating s'mores. The girls did not know that I had been close to drowning. They never knew how close death had been to all of us.

Within a few months the winds of grief would, without warning, sweep into my life and plunge me deep into another, more treacherous storm.

IN THE BEGINNING

November 2, 1952

My mother Jessymae Martin waddled through the side door of the Mapleton Evangelical United Brethren Church, donned her maroon choir robe, and climbed the stairs into the choir loft. She lowered her tiny body, swollen with child, into the organ which was nestled between the pews. The congregation could barely see the top of her head as she began playing the prelude. At some point between the beginning of the sermon and the closing hymn, her water broke. She whispered this information to one of the sopranos who instructed a few men from the tenor and bass section to help unwedge her from the organ, and soon, Dad was at her side.

Dad handed my 18-month-old brother Larry to their babysitter Verona Taylor. He and Mom sped off for Sacred Heart Hospital in Eugene. Two hours after Mom had played the final chord of the Benediction, I entered the world and my brother's position as the most important person in the world had been usurped. After my brother's birth Mom had been told by her doctor, due to her physical frailty, not to have another pregnancy. I was obviously a "mistake" and I doubt that my birth was greeted with the same amount of joy and hope with which they had greeted their firstborn son.

My father wanted my brother to have all the successes, achievements and comforts possible to him. Dad had been raised during the Depression and he was determined to ensure that Larry would become a well-educated and capable breadwinner. My brother was assigned errands, he learned to build fires in the Boy Scouts, he was taught to play chess, and he was taught how to put a worm on a hook. I took violin lessons, learned to knit in Girl Scouts, and played piano for church. Larry was required to find a summer job when he was in high school, but my parents would not allow me to pursue summer employment. I was told that it wasn't necessary to work, so I spent my summers swimming, hanging out with friends and getting a good tan. Larry had good reason to feel some resentment.

When I expressed a desire to learn chess, I was told, "chess isn't for girls". When I begged to accompany my father and brother on their many fishing trips, I was told "girls are bad luck." Once Dad asked Larry to go fly fishing on the Siuslaw River and Larry refused to go. Dad looked crushed, sad that his only son would not go fishing with him. I eagerly said, "I'll go Daddy!" He turned to me and said, "okay, let's go". I spent the morning sitting on the banks of the river, watching him cast his line into the water. I don't remember if he caught any fish. It soon became apparent that boys had more fun than girls, and I wanted to be a boy.

I mostly played alone as a child. Occasionally I would join my brother and his friends as they played cowboys and Indians. This seldom ended well. I was usually appointed to be the "Indian" which meant that, in the end, I was tied to the tether-ball pole with ropes and taunted. Sometimes I was even punched.

I spent my time reading and making up plays, which I acted out in front of an audience of dolls and teddy bears. I played dress-up and made up songs. As I got older, I wrote play scripts and poems that nobody in my family wanted to hear. I wrote "The Mystery of Mars" when I was eleven years old and my Girl Scout Troop wore green dyed bed sheets as they performed my one-act play in the Grange Hall. I never once dreamed of being a wife or a mother.

December 16, 1957

Excerpt from Christmas Letter from the Martins:

> *"Phyllis is quite a lively five-year old. She has accepted Larry's going to school with complete calm and seems quite content to stay home and be mama's little girl. Her main activity is changing clothes fifteen times a day and being just Phyllis. She has a lot of ability to find things to do to amuse herself."*

As I entered puberty, the feminist movement was well on its way and I heard about women becoming doctors and lawyers. There was even a story about women burning their bras for some reason. Women all over the country were making the statement that they were of equal worth to men. I agreed with the feminist platform, but messages on the home front were confusing. What did it mean to be a woman?

Back when my mother was twenty-one years-old she was a 6th grade teacher in Shedd, Oregon and she learned that the male teacher in the adjacent room was being paid twice the amount of her wage. She complained to the school superintendent who told her, "Sorry you're a woman and he is a man who has a family to feed." In spite of that experience, my mother did not openly support female equality. She continued to believe until she was in her 70's that women should not be pastors, doctors, or lawyers. She also believed that, as a woman, she could never be complete without my father.

I don't understand how my mother, a teacher, could acquiesce to the notion that I would just wander with little direction into some sort of acceptable and maybe even meaningful adulthood. She shared with me many years later that she considered her decision to become a teacher as "selfish." She felt she should have been a housewife so my brother and I could walk through the door after school and be greeted with a plate of warm chocolate chip cookies.

I had a supremely happy childhood despite this gender inequity and lack of direction, and I was obliviously content. My mother was unreasonably attentive while Father admired me from afar as his precocious talented daughter. But I have an early memory of sitting on my father's lap while he visited with a friend. He said to his friend (as if I was deaf), "she's very cute but she'll never be very smart".

My brother and I took IQ tests when we were in the fifth and sixth grades. I do not know what the scores looked like or whether we performed within the average or high average ranges. Our parents did not share the results with us because, as I found out decades later,

I had obtained a higher score than Larry. They didn't want him to feel bad about himself. They did, however, allow me to believe I wasn't very smart.

Why do two individuals, raised in the same home, grow up to have opposing sets of values and beliefs? How can a brother and sister have the same experience and walk away with different memories? Today my brother and I live in two separate worlds. His memories of childhood differ significantly from mine and if he were writing about our family, one would hardly recognize that we were raised by the same parents, in the same home. But this is MY story.

JUNE 1958

THE PERFECT FAMILY

Mother had been pampered as a child, primarily due to her status as the youngest child, and more importantly, because she was physically disabled due to Juvenile Rheumatoid Arthritis. Her mother would not allow her to perform any household chores. As a result, Mother didn't know how to cook. Regardless, she was determined to become the perfect housewife due to popular television shows about intact nuclear families. The bar was set fairly high on television shows where the mother wore a dress and heels all the time, kissed the father goodbye at the door each morning, and greeted the children with a plate of warm cookies when they ran through the door after school. The mother was almost always in the kitchen. "Father Knows Best" was very popular but I remember thinking, "no he doesn't."

Mother subscribed to a variety of magazines including, Good Housekeeping, Better Homes and Gardens, and Ladies Home Journal. They contained recipes for casseroles made with Campbell's Cream-of-Something soup: tuna, chicken, hamburger casseroles. We ate dinner together every night and afterwards we would watch the news, which at the time was just the news: Information about what was happening in the world, with no commentary and no opinions.

When I was in grade school images from the civil rights movement began to flash across the screen with increasing frequency. I recall seeing a segment about a little black girl being escorted to school by police as angry white adults screamed and spit on her. I saw Black people being sprayed with fire hoses and attacked by ferocious dogs. I saw thousands of Black people marching across a bridge. I watched with confusion as more white people screamed and threw rocks, and I recall hearing Martin Luther King articulately speaking about equality and peaceful protest, and God. I would like to tell you that after watching the news, Dad would gather us around to discuss civil rights issues. But he didn't. We continued to just quietly watch the news without commentary and then wander off to our rooms. Or we would remain seated on the couch as Father turned the channel to Father Knows Best.

MAPLETON

Mapleton is a little logging town nestled in the coast range, situated along both sides of the Siuslaw River. Our town had its own little valley, thick with Maple trees (hence the name of the town), ferns, berry bushes and luscious forests of fir trees. A beautiful covered bridge spanned the river, and it was a majestic edifice, the symbol of Mapleton. During the Fall, a canopy of bright orange and red maple leaves would further define the river. Mapleton had a post office, two bars, three restaurants, an automotive garage, a Lions Club, an Elks Lodge, a beauty shop, a barber shop, two grocery stores and, of course, a school. The Evangelical United Brethren Church, situated on the north side of the river, was the only church in town.

My parents moved to Mapleton in 1947 to teach school. Father was hired as the high school math and science teacher while Mother taught the sixth grade. Father was eventually promoted to Superintendent of Schools and he joined the wealthy business owners as one of the most dynamic, influential, and progressive leaders in town. Mother was church organist, choir director, and was active in multiple civic organizations. Over time, they became an integral part of the community.

The Martin family stood out as an exemplary family of the era. Our two parent/two children configuration attended Sunday school and church every Sunday. We lived in a new house (built the year I was born), had a late model car, went out of state for summer vacations, my brother and I had braces, and I took private violin and piano lessons. Life was filled with swim lessons, scout camp, and vacation bible school. Holidays and birthdays were celebrated with freshly baked cakes, cookies, gaudy decorations, gifts, Fostoria glassware, chiffon dresses, patented leather shoes and lacy hats. Mother had center pieces and decorations not only for Christmas, but also for Valentine's Day (red and white streamers, red construction paper hearts), Easter (flowers, linen tablecloth, Easter eggs, baskets, and stuffed rabbits), Halloween (carved jack-o-lanterns, black and orange streamers, chocolate cupcakes with orange icing and candy corn perched in the middle, napkin ghosts made with tootsie-roll pops with napkins wrapped around the top, cut-out witches, black cats, and goblins taped to the inside of the windows) and Thanksgiving (accordion-paper turkeys and a bouquet of gold and red maple leaves).

Christmas began the Friday after Thanksgiving. A confusing array of religious symbolism clashed with secular icons, as Rudolph stood next to baby Jesus in the manger and Santa's sleigh sat under the Eastern Star. Windows were stenciled with white powdered outlines of snowflakes and a "fireplace" consisted of a small desk wound in corrugated paper with black and red brick designs. We were by all accounts, the perfect family.

On September 9, 1956, Mom told me that guests were coming and that I had to go to bed. I could hear the door open and close as people began to arrive and, although they spoke with hushed voices, I knew there was a small crowd gathering in our living room. I hopped out of bed and crept down the hall. About ten adults were gathered around the television set watching Elvis sing "You Ain't Nothin' but a Hound Dog" on The Ed Sullivan Show. A few months earlier our cousin Blair, who worked at Western Auto in Florence, had delivered a television set. (The first time I heard a cuss word was when Blair got an electrical shock while installing our television set.) All these people were in our home because we had one of the only televisions in town.

We were different than many of our neighbors who relied on the fickle timber industry for survival. Business was booming in the 50's and 60's for logging companies and lumber mills and the owners of these operations were understandably the most influential men in town. A separate socioeconomic class included shop owners and, of course, educators.   I was clueless regarding any class distinction. I was unaware of the unique social position held by the Martins, and oblivious to poverty. When I was in the first grade, I noticed that some children were poorly groomed and sometimes emitted a strange odor. They were not good students and their eyes were empty and gaunt. Like Laura. She sometimes smelled like popcorn, her hair was stringy and oily, and her face was dirty. Her eyes were dark and haunted, and she rarely spoke. I was somewhat disturbed by Laura, but at the same time felt very sorry for her when the other children made fun of her.

Several years later when I was nine years old, snow began to fall during recess. It rarely snowed in Mapleton and when it did, school was often cancelled. This meant that I would get to stay home, play in the snow, and drink hot chocolate. I was thrilled! But I could see that James, a fellow fourth grader, was frowning. "Aren't you happy it's snowing?" I asked. He sadly replied, "you wouldn't be happy either if you had holes in your shoes."

The farther away a family lived from town, the more likely it was they lived in a shack with no electricity or running water. There were few social programs in place then to ensure that basic physical needs were being met for those in need of assistance and teachers, including my mother, would, on occasion, send clothing and food home with the children. No one talked about it. It was just what it was. Meanwhile, I blithely lived in a little cocoon in our comfortable home overlooking the river, up on a hill in the forest. I did not know that our family was privileged.

14

WHAT DO YOU WANT TO BE WHEN YOU GROW UP?

When I was about four years of age, I became very ill. There was no doctor in Mapleton, and hospitals were for broken bones and people who were at Death's door, so Mother called a nurse who lived in town and asked that she come see me. When she knocked on the door, mother said, "the nurse is here" with a hint of hope and reverence in her voice. My parents and the nurse spoke in hushed voices for a few minutes. Then the nurse quietly stepped into my bedroom and sat on the edge of my bed. She wore white and spoke with soft, gentle, firm tones as she asked me how I was feeling. She placed a cool washcloth on my forehead, stroked my head and gave me some medication. I felt safe with her, and her presence assured me that everything was going to be fine. I knew then that I wanted to be just like her.

Several years later our family went to Disneyland when I was ten years old. We decided to split up and meet in an hour. (That's how things were in 1962. Parents just assumed their kids would be able to independently navigate the chaotic streets of Disneyland on a hot fourth of July afternoon and be just fine). Suddenly I heard a woman desperately calling for help: "Please! Someone help my little girl". I rounded the corner to see an African American woman kneeling next to a little girl who was lying unconscious on the ground. I watched as a crowd of white faces gathered, but no one stepped forward to help. No one. I wanted so badly to help, but I didn't know what to do. I just stood and stared with the rest of the crowd. I finally turned away and began to walk toward the Matterhorn where our family had agreed to meet up. I told myself that someday I would be the person who would tend to that little girl lying on the ground. I would have compassion and empathy and I would know what to do. And I would do it without hesitation.

YOU'RE GOOD AT THAT!

No one asked me what I wanted to be when I grew up. My parents never had a discussion with me about my professional aspirations although there was an unspoken assumption that music would somehow play a part in my future. I played "Jesus Loves Me" on the piano by ear when I was four years old and began taking private violin lessons when I was eight The pastor's wife was my first piano teacher. I did not like her because she wouldn't let me play by ear. Mrs. Devitto, the grade school music teacher, was certain that I was destined for Julliard. When company came I loved how my father's eyes would light up when I played, and I learned that, in order to gain his affection, I would need to perform well.

I attended a summer orchestra music camp at the University of Oregon when I was twelve years old and by the last day of camp, I knew I didn't want to be a professional musician.   Lorna Kowalski (my roommate) and I were assigned to the 2nd violin section, seated towards the back row but we didn't care because we were there to have a good time. I had only played my violin as a soloist and had never played in an orchestra. Music camp was a foreign experience for me: The other students bragged about their abilities and accomplishments, seemed to be wound tight with no sense of humor, and fiercely competed for the best chair in the orchestra. I, however, played the violin because it was fun, and I didn't care how my musical proficiency compared with other violinists.

If being a professional musician meant that I would have to associate with these music snobs, I wanted nothing of it. I told Mother that I did not want to play music professionally upon my return from camp. There was no more discussion about my future, except for the assumption that I would attend Oregon State University after graduating from high school. My father thought that it would be a good experience and I think that he assumed that Oregon State would be a good place to find a husband.

FREEDOM IN PARADISE

Childhood was a time of tremendous freedom. I freely biked down our hill and across the covered bridge to visit friends, hiked through the woods, walked to town to meet friends at Schultz's bar for a Shirley Temple and fries, and explored the forest. When I was five years old a bulldozer broke through the trees behind our home. Houses eventually sprang up on either side of the dirt road by our house which led up the hill to the Projects where the Plywood Mill employees lived. I swam for hours without restraint on hot summer days in the slow lazy Siuslaw River. My mother would drop my brother and me with our sack lunches at the Lions Club Dock at around 11:00 in the morning and return around 3:00. There were no lifeguards, no adults, just a bunch of children of various ages who looked out for one another. No one was ever hurt, and no one ever drowned. We would go to Mrs. Johnson's house across the street and stand dripping wet on her porch if we needed a Band-Aid.

I was eventually allowed to bike downtown at night and our gaggle of friends would run through the covered bridge, sit in the windows, and watch cars and trucks as they rumbled by. We had no watches and no strict guidance about where we could go or when we should be home. No one worried about kidnapping, human trafficking, or sexual assault. Those words were not in our vocabulary.

YOU'RE GOING TO HELL

I began my religious life when I was an infant, in the nursery of the Evangelical United Brethren (EUB) Church of Mapleton. I shared a crib with Mark Hess with whom I would eventually attend the Homecoming Dance our first year of high school. The EUB church rose out of the holiness movement of the early century and embraced the belief in heaven, hell, a god of justice and a Jesus of forgiveness and love. The Holy Spirit was a genderless entity who would cause you to feel guilty when you sinned, and, at some point, this Holy Spirit would "come into" you to help you live a righteous life. I grew up in the church memorizing bible verses, praying, and striving to be a good Christian.

Our family attended church every Sunday where Mother played the organ and taught Sunday school. I learned that Jesus loved me, and we sang lots of songs. The church also taught that: 1) Every word of the Bible is true. Every word. No questions allowed; 2) There is a Heaven and a Hell; 3) You can only go to Heaven if you believe in Jesus; and 4) Everyone else is going to Hell.

Every year an evangelist would come for one week of "Revival" services beginning on Sunday night and ending on Friday night. The sermons focused on the need for salvation by Jesus Christ and If you weren't saved, you were going to hell. The altar in the front of the church was where you went to be "saved". The first time I "went to the altar" I was seven years old. I didn't know why, but I felt very sad as the congregants sang the final hymn. As others made their way to the altar, like a lemming, I went to the altar too. When I began to cry the evangelist asked me why I was crying, and I told him that my mother was sick. He asked the pianist to stop playing the hymn and announced that the church would now pray for my ailing mother who, incidentally, was at home watching Bonanza.

But you had to do more than believe in Jesus. You had to:

- Accept Him as your personal savior
- Believe He was from a virgin birth
- Believe He is God incarnate
- Believe He died on the cross and rose again
- Believe humans are inherently evil and Jesus is the only one who can rid us of that evil.
- AND, if you are not careful you could accidentally sin (i.e. get mad at your brother) and boom! You could accidentally lose your salvation and go to hell.

I wondered about all the people in other countries, like those who pray to Buddha. What about people who simply haven't heard about Jesus? The answer was: missionaries need to be sent. You just need to go tell all those gazillions of other people about Jesus so they won't go to Hell, oh, by the way, the Bible says when all the people have heard about Jesus, He will come again in the clouds and we will all go to Heaven.

The notion of Jesus appearing in the clouds and everyone floating up to Heaven was quite unnerving. His Coming would also be fairly disruptive, but I was a good Christian girl and wanted to believe it all and I decided to become a missionary. Correction, a missionary's wife. My husband would preach, and I would play the piano, and all the natives would joyfully accept Jesus and dance. Not sinful dancing. Psalms dancing.

Every night I knelt by my bed to say my prayers. I prayed for the people I cared about and for those who I wanted to be kept safe. I would also pray for forgiveness, not for anything in particular, but just to cover my bases. I would ask Jesus to return that night because if I asked for forgiveness right before I went to sleep that meant I would go to Heaven if he came during the night. Just in case tomorrow I might accidentally sin, get run over by a truck or get hit with lightening, and accidentally go to Hell.

My parents did not know that I was becoming emotionally and spiritually damaged. Mom and Dad attended this church because it was the only Protestant church in town and they only went to Sunday morning services. Mom had been raised in the Christian Church, tried to read her Bible every day, and was confident that she would go to Heaven. Dad had been raised in a small Nazarene church and had been exposed to bizarre demonstrative displays in church attributed to the "moving" of the Holy Spirit. He was repulsed by any demonstration of overt religiosity or emotional outbursts and believed that the Bible, written by men over the centuries, was meant to be a spiritual guide. My parents did not join me as I attended the Bible studies, prayer meetings, evangelical services, and summer evangelical camps where church dogma was on full display. My parents had no idea how afraid I was of God.

When I was about 11 years old, the pastor asked two of the young men in church wearing military uniforms to stand so we could pray for them. They were on their way to Vietnam. The pastor prayed that they would "vanquish the enemy, kill the evil soldiers, and obliterate the North Vietnamese." That was rather confusing. "Jesus loves me, thou shalt not kill......but go kill people?" I suppose that was the moment my theological underpinnings began to falter.

THE TRAINWRECK AND WHY I BELIEVE THERE IS A GOD

It was a hot August day in 1962 when Mother and I drove up Cemetery Hill to deliver a meal to Mrs. Jensen, a sick friend of my mother's. As we drove back down the hill in our old 1958 Ford, we chatted about how I would soon be entering the sixth grade.

Mother slowed the car as we approached the railroad tracks at the bottom of the hill. I looked to my right and saw a train bearing down on us and, as I screamed, Mom tried to put the car in reverse. The engine died and the car rolled on to the tracks. I heard the sharp metal and brakes grinding as I lunged over to the driver's side. The train caught the right front fender and dragged us about 30 feet until it stopped.

Mom steadied me as I climbed out the driver's window into the arms of a sloppy fat man wearing soiled striped bibbed overalls. He held me tight and seemed reluctant to put me down and I decided that he must be the engineer. He smelled of strong body odor, cigarettes and alcohol and repeatedly asked me, "are you okay little girl?" My only thought was, "please put me down!"

Miraculously, neither of us were injured. The door had been ripped from the passenger side, but the car still ran. So Mother, as pragmatic as she was, decided to continue home with a stop at the grocery store. I was still dazed, and when I saw a fellow classmate in the store, I told him that I had just been hit by a train. He just stared at me and walked away. I would understand when I was much older that others don't really want to hear your bad news, nor do they know what to say when you try to tell them your problems.

We didn't talk about the wreck at all after that, but when Dad got home, I peeked through the crack of my bedroom door as Mom cried on his shoulder saying, "oh Claude, we could've been killed!" I

25

stayed in my room and read a Woody the Woodpecker comic book over and over again. I couldn't stop reading, even though I recognized this as aberrant behavior, even for me. I must've read that book for three hours, mechanically reading each page, memorizing each word. I now understand that this was a post-trauma soothing behavior. I don't recall if Dad came in to see if I was okay. I suppose since there were no broken bones, everyone assumed all was well.

Two weeks later, I was home alone with Mother when she told me she was driving to the grocery store and would be right back. I heard the car back out of the driveway and at the same time, I heard a train whistle coming from the west. I was worried that she would reach the tracks at the bottom of the hill just as the train got to our road. "These Boots Were Made For Walkin'" by Nancy Sinatra was playing on the stereo turntable. I panicked as I listened for the crash and began to silently pray, "God, if Mom is alright, make the record skip." I prayed with great earnest and fervor and suddenly, the record began to skip. I was frightened and amazed. I slowly looked around the room expecting to see an angel, or maybe even Jesus, but I was alone. I slowly walked to the stereo and gently removed the skipping needle from the record. I cautiously knelt next to the hassock and prayed, "thank you." Since then I have questioned the nature of God, and I have, now and then, turned my back on organized religion. However, except for a very brief time, I have never had any doubt that a God, a Someone, a Him or Her, a mysterious Entity is present in my world.

BOOK 1

PART I: THE DIARIES

1963 – 1969

THE DIARIES

I received my first diary for my 11th birthday on November 2, 1963.

November 2: Today is my birthday, Saturday 1963. I first went to the school with Daddy to get the bull out of the schoolyard. Then we went to Florence, and when we got back, I had a surprise party!

November 9: I started writing a play tonight. It's called "The Mystery of Mars".

November 11: We went to Eugene and the teacher let me play her violin! Bobby Sneddon (my cousin) slept on my lap on the way back. Today was Veteran's Day.

November 22: Today a very tragic thing happened. Our president died, he was assassinated. President John F. Kennedy was killed by a rifle shot - in the head. People didn't react like you would expect them to. People just stood around and wept. The story goes that he was riding in a convertible when someone shot three shots at him. One missed, but two hit him in the head. One of the other bullets hit the governor of Texas. I wish this day would end. I just can't believe it!

Our teacher Mrs. Cowell tearfully delivered the news to our class that President Kennedy was dead. Then we numbly filed through the school halls, up to the high school gym where all the students, grade school through high school, were gathering. One eight grade boy said, "good, I'm glad he's dead. He was a terrible president". Several boys attacked with him their fists and we just continued walking toward the gym where my father, as the superintendent of schools, announced what we already knew to be true.

November 23: Today was gloomy as yesterday, people aren't interested in other news; a very big fire killed 63 old people at an old people's home, and nobody cares!

November 25: Today Larry and I played monopoly. Then we went on a hike. We packed a lunch and were gone for two hours. We got a million things and made a fairy land out of them. Today was John F. Kennedy's funeral.

We returned to school a few days after the funeral of our president. When we returned to school, there was no more mention of our nation's loss. Although the future of our country had been forever altered, no counseling was offered. I do not recall my parents comforting me or even saying much about it. The only implied acknowledgement was when we sat as a family in front of the television watching the funeral procession, crying as little John saluted the casket as it rumbled by. The adults assumed that the children would be just fine. It was 1963, and it would be decades before psychologists would begin to study the effects of collective traumatization.

DETECTIVES

I was impressed with the Hardy Boys (I had the entire set: ten blue bound books). The colorful escapades about two teenage boys solving mysteries intrigued me.

December 3: Peggy Kilpatrick and I have started a new club. It is a detective club. Peggy has a finger-printer. I have a magnifying glass. We went to town a bought 25 pieces of bubblegum.

I'm not sure what buying bubblegum had to do with being a detective, but I'm sure it made sense at the time. I didn't write regularly in my diary for quite a few months, and when I did, it was a boring menu of what I had done that day:

December 24: This morning I woke up and looked under the stockings. There was a new violin! Oh it sounds nice! There was also a stuffed chipmunk . I named it Tweak because it squeaks when you squeeze the tail.

1964

February 1: We went to church today. Then Mom fried chicken and we watched Bonanza.

June 10: We went swimming today! We stayed at the dock all day and I got a real bad sunburn! I think Eddie likes me!

BOYS

I started noticing boys when I was eleven years old. One Spring day, John Lehman and I walked the perimeter of the playground holding hands during recess. We were scolded by the fifth-grade teacher Mrs. Southwick (of course we called her Mrs. South Witch), who told us we should know better. I guess we didn't. The sixth grade was a romantically busy year for me. Guy Bennet and I passed love notes in class. He also gave me a necklace of beads, which I promptly lost. He was an American Indian and those beads were probably significant or maybe even worth some money. In one of those love notes we agreed to meet "over the hill" to kiss. The cafeteria was literally *over a hill* which we hiked each day at lunchtime.

Anyway, I was headed to lunch, and he jumped out from behind a bush, planted a sloppy kiss on my cheek, and ran off. That was that.

August 18: When I came home from school, I was supposed to go to Florence, but Dad and Larry went golfing. (Dad's birthday). I got a tie tack for him down at Beck's store. Then Sneddons and Aunt Emma came up tonight. Reta, Mike, Tommy, Donny, Larry, and I played kick the can. It was really fun. Aunt Emma stayed over.

November 28: The Campbells came up today, because it was Thanksgiving. We had a large turkey. Then we, I mean Calvin, Larry, Hope, and I, played monopoly. We ate a whole cake! We went into the (travel) trailer house and played Pit, Clue, Sorry, and Monopoly till 12:00, at night! Hope and I slept together and talked and scratched backs till 2:00.

1965

February 14: Valentine's Day! What a day for Billy and Peg to break up! I wonder if Jerry still likes Anne. Kids say he doesn't but I'm hoping for Anne. I get to go to My Fair Lady on Thursday. I hope Rusty goes!

February 25: You should have seen Rusty, Robbie, and Pam and I tonight at the ball game. They both had their arms around me. It was a mess! So, the rumor's around that I was up there making out and I wasn't.

March 4: Rusty walked me to the bus! I like him a lot more than I do Eddie.

March 15: I went to the barn with Peggy. Everyone was wrestling in the hay and the boys were trying to "pants" the girls. I was mad and just went over to a little cubbyhole and sat down. Pretty soon Rusty was with me. He told me he was going to get me a ring! I guess he wants to go steady.

I was uncomfortably wearing a two-piece swimming suit and was swimming at Pennel's dock when Rusty Holman grabbed the back of my top as I was jumping into the water. My top flew off as I ducked under the dock to hide as he laughed at me. I don't know how I got out. Apparently, based on the previous entries, I had a crush on Rusty Holman.

I continued to write almost daily. Unfortunately, my diaries from remainder of 1965 and 1966 were lost somewhere between Oregon to Alaska to Oregon to Iowa and back to Oregon.

UNWELCOME CHANGES

Kathy Sullivan and Kathy Carriveau were slathered in Coppertone baking in the sun on the Pennel's dock on the river. Just lying there. I didn't get it. Why weren't they swimming? I knew I was missing something, that I was out of step. We were all out of step. There are no secure footholds for puberty.

Mom graduated from Eastern Oregon State College in August 1965. Teachers had previously been required to obtain a 3-year education certification, but by 1965 all teachers were required to complete a bachelor's degree. She had been taking classes in Eugene. Our family was driving to La Grande, her former alma mater, to attend her graduation.

I was twelve years old and Mom had purchased me a bra and nylons. Pantyhose had not been invented so I had to wear a "garter belt" (essentially a belt with four straps which attached to nylons). My period had started a few months earlier and I was aware that I was beginning to develop breasts. I did not appreciate any of these changes and found it all to be very inconvenient. Mom helped me put the nylons and bra on, and I stood, looking in the motel mirror, feeling....just strange. I was acutely aware in this moment of clarity that my childhood was fading away. A wave of somber contemplation swept over me as I understood that I had begun my journey into womanhood. I did not like it one bit.

THE VIET NAM WAR

We began to watch the News from Viet Nam on our television (in living color!) when I was about 13 years old. We witnessed young soldiers on stretchers; a little naked girl on fire, running away from the camera; coffins draped with the American Flag; newsmen breathlessly reporting about casualties, bombed villages, and devastation. The reporters spoke into the camera as they stood in front of muddy army tanks and they talked with dirty rumpled soldiers barely older than my brother - young boys with weary eyes and empty faces, smoking cigarettes. The political tide began to turn as Americans watched the horrors of war play out in their living rooms. Our family rarely discussed the news but one day Dad, a WWII veteran, said that this was a bad war and that our young men were dying "for nothing".

1967

DISCRIMINATION

August 8: Leon called tonight, and we talked for a long time. He's really lonely and has a lot of problems. I really think he's nice.

August 13, 1967: Leon sang in the choir today. He's a really good singer!

I had never seen a Black human being in person until Leon came to town. He was in his teens, was in the Job Corps and worked with a crew of young men assigned to some sort of project in the woods.

Leon came to church and sang in the choir. We became friends and one day he secretly kissed me lightly on the cheek when we said goodbye. When he came to my house to visit, Mother turned him away at the door. Later I would hear that he had been ambushed by a bunch of high school boys who threw rocks at him and punched him in the face as he walked by the school. Unfortunately, Oregon has a history of overt prejudicial policy against African Americans and has historically been a very "white" state. When Dad bought our home from Mr. Wright in 1962, the contract specified that the home would never be sold to a "Negro". Years later Mother spoke of the moment she saw Leon on our porch. She said, "I don't know why I turned him away, I still feel bad about it."

RUSTY

September 15: Today I feel rather tired, and kind of happy, but not so happy. This is how you feel when you want something to happen and it doesn't. I was at Rusty's last night, so I don't think I'll do very well on the math test tomorrow. I hope Rusty doesn't like me. He would have to be stupid to like me.

September 27: Rusty asked me to the prom Sunday! I couldn't believe it!

I was in love with Rusty. He had red hair and blue eyes and lived with his mother who was divorced from his alcoholic dad. He wasn't a good student, but I loved him. He lived across from Pam Souder who lived with her widowed dad who either slept or was never home. She was a good friend and it was all quite convenient. I attended the Homecoming Dance (almost as important as the Spring Prom) with Rusty. I wore a rust-colored velour floor length dress, hand sewn by Mrs. Moore, the local seamstress. In the dating world, going to homecoming together was almost as official as a formal engagement announcement.

But remember the Jesus thing? Rusty didn't attend church, and he said "damn" on occasion. He was going to Hell according to the teachings of my church and I had no business dating him. In late September under a clear night sky I stood alone in Pam Souder's front yard and whispered aloud to the stars. "God, if he's not a Christian by January I'll break up with him."

November 2: Today is my birthday. Wow. I'm 15 years old today. Rusty made me mad. He got drunk Tuesday night (Halloween). He got me a stuffed dog. It's cute.

November 20: Rusty and I are doing just dandy. Why do I like him so much? He's certainly not good for me, heaven knows!

By January, I had stopped kneeling for prayer every night (or any night). I was going to church, but I had only one thing on my mind.

1968

January 1: I went over to Pam's today. We walked around the block and over the Rusty's. Pam left and I suppose I should've gone with her, but we don't get to be alone too often. I love Rusty.

January 12: Rusty and I had a spat. He is very embarrassing at times, and very depressing.

January 28: I went to Rusty's. He said he loves me very much. He and I were on his bed and his hand got moving a little too much. I asked him if he thought I was cheap. He said, "not if you don't do this with anyone else". So I guess I'll marry him. I love him.

February 7: Rusty got his license! I'm so happy. Now we can be together, alone. And go together to places. Alone!

February 12: Terrible night! My cupcakes were ruined, Mom said I couldn't go to Florence with Rusty, and I can't go to any more dances if Hippies play and no one would listen to me at the table.

37

February 14: Rusty took me to Florence then he took me to the Gingerbread Village to get a milkshake. Then he gave me six red long-stemmed rose buds! I was so happy I could've died! The card says, "To the sweetest girl in the world". I love him very much!

We found ourselves alone in his bedroom around Valentine's day. We didn't have sex. But it was close. And I asked him, "What are we going to do?" I may have said something about marriage, I don't know, but I began to concoct a plan. We could elope, I could sell my snow skis, steal the family car and we would ride off into wherever it is stupid teenagers in love go.

February 17: Rusty and I rode the rooter's bus home from the Newport game. I love him very very very very very very much. And I sincerely mean that. I will love him the rest of my life, I just know it! I just can't be wrong! It's too good a thing. I love him too much. We're getting married after we're out of college. I love him!

In the following days he didn't seem to be around very much. He had his license now, and I would see his car around town, often parked at Reta Ware's house.

March 4: This has been the most miserable day I have ever had in my entire life. Rusty didn't say one word to me. I bawled all day.

March 8: He ignored me again today but picked me up for the dance at 9:15 tonight. It started okay until he asked if he could dance with Reta. Then on the way out he nudged her. This whole thing just gets worse by the minute.

March 13: Rusty came over and everything is just fine. He kissed me and I did a bad thing. I said "Damn you" to Rusty. Rusty said Micky and Reta did it and tried to talk me into doing it. No dice. He stayed until 2:30 A.M. and he gave me three hickeys.

If I have learned anything at all in life, it is that DENIAL is one of the most durable defense mechanisms employed by the human psyche.

In March, Rusty's friend approached me in the school hallway by the gym and across from my father's office. Robbie Roberts had a crush on me, so I was skeptical when he told me that Rusty had a message for me. "Rusty says he's going to dedicate a song to you (in the school paper). It's called *Breaking Up Is Hard to Do*." I brushed it off because it was just Robbie and I was in denial. That evening I was seated on the third row of bleachers waiting for the basketball game to begin when a friend nudged me and pointed up to the couple seated a few rows behind us. It was Rusty and Reta. He was holding her hand and she was wearing his letterman's jacket as he gave her his class ring.

March 20: Oh my! We broke up today. His idea. Went to game tonight. Saw Rusty sitting with Reta holding her hand and exchanging rings. I started crying. Oh, it killed me. I am deeply hurt. In fact, I'm crying right now. I'll try to get through tomorrow. Oh help. He's gone.

How can I describe how it feels to have a heart suddenly break? (I feel sad just writing this 49 years later). I ran to the girl's bathroom, fell prone on the floor, and began to sob. Then I vomited. How could he hurt me like this? How could Reta do this? I would never turn on another person like this. I was ironing clothes for school that night and realized, "nothing matters anymore".   I looked in my closet to lay out my clothes for the next day and thought, "it doesn't matter what I wear, nothing matters."   I had become singularly focused on Rusty. All my decisions hinged on pleasing him, looking pretty for him, and existing for him. But what about God? My heart was broken, and I was going to Hell.

March 23:   *I've searched but I can't find, I've looked but I can't see*
             I've listened but He hasn't had a thing to say to me.
             My eyes have asked the skies where He might be.
             Perhaps He is just hiding from me to let me be Damned for
             eternity.
             I've asked but no answers come to me.

Are you there God?
A mist has covered me and I can no longer see.

Many years later, my mother revealed that she had considered seeking professional help for me at the time because I was so distraught. I'm glad she didn't. Psychiatric treatment was crude and often ineffective in 1968 and anything could have happened: I could have been labeled with an inaccurate psychiatric diagnosis; I could have become inappropriately medicated; or I may have even been given a lobotomy.

I attended a class reunion in August 2000, and there he was standing on the lawn, his red hair tied back in a ponytail at the nape of his neck. He looked good. Strong, nice physique. My heart skipped a beat. I walked towards him and I said, "Rusty Holman you broke my heart!" And we began to visit about our kids, our lives, and where the road had taken us. It turns out his road took him to a wife, children, jail, and an automotive garage. As we talked, I realized that his IQ was probably a bit lower than mine. But I'll bet he's good in bed.

WILD CHILD

I questioned my self-worth after Rusty broke up with me even though I was a good student, an impressive musician, and a good friend to many. However, I had been rejected, I believed, for being who I was. I was a nerd: I was studious, never got in trouble, played violin, had braces on my teeth and wore pointy black glasses. I was, however, casual friends with many of my fellow students including the cheerleaders and jocks. (I shared the title of "friendliest girl" with Debbie Skinner during my senior year. I was also voted as the girl having "the biggest feet"). Before losing Rusty, none of these things mattered. I decided that my image as a "good girl" had to change, so I began forging new friendships with the girls who broke the rules.

March 22: I'm staying with Kathyrn tonight. So is Sherrie. Kath and I split a beer and I can honestly say that I have never tasted worse stuff in my life! He's gone. I loved him. It's like Brutus (Reta) and Caesar (me). We stayed up till 4:30.

The first time I attended a kegger I got drunk. I gagged on the first sip of beer, so I held my nose and chugged it down until I began to feel the effects of alcohol. After a few more glasses I was not myself anymore and I no longer felt sad or guilty. When I went into the bathroom, I looked at myself in the mirror and said, aloud, "you are going to hell". It felt so good to feel numb and to not hurt anymore.

The next morning my mother talked to me about how she had "heard" (someone had called her) about the party. She voiced her concern that I could be so easily swayed into behaving so poorly. She clarified that, as Martins, this was unacceptable behavior. Naturally I promised I would never drink alcohol or, in any other way, behave so dishonorably again. Now I needed to be more careful and secretive about future exploits. I did not begin getting drunk every weekend, nor did I start having indiscriminate sex. However, I did take advantage of the occasional opportunity to imbibe.

Mom decided after school was out that it would be fun for me to go camping at Cleowox State Park with some of my girlfriends. My father pulled our little camper trailer to a camp site, and arranged for my cousin's husband Blair, who lived closer to the campground, to be the emergency contact person.

June 24: Went camping with Deb L., Deb S., and Paula D. This guy from Florence is staying with us and the cops are after him! There's a lot more I could say but it's too tiring!

June 25: State Fuzz came by today. So did the Park Ranger. So did Mom and Geraldine. We had to go home.

Paula Pendegrass had invited herself along and notified one of her boyfriends that we would be there for the weekend. Unfortunately, several other boys appeared at the campsite with him. They had all been stealing from the campsites during the previous week and were wanted by the police. Adult beverages were, of course, involved and Blair was not happy when he received a phone call at 5:00 A.M. from the police. He had had several wisdom teeth pulled the previous day and was not feeling his best, so this was an especially inconvenient time for him to be disturbed. We girls received some sort of admonishment from the policeman and Blair. Mom and my cousin Geraldine (Blair's wife) were there to retrieve us by 8:00. To this day Blair never fails to remind me about how he saved my hide.

June 29: I was laying in the sun today and Rusty and Mike snuck up on me and tried to rape me! They had my pants half-way down and Larry came around the corner, so they stopped.

Larry did come upon us, but really didn't "stop" them. He said, very calmly, "guys, that's probably not a very good idea". It hurt me that he wasn't mad. Weren't big brothers supposed to protect their little sisters?

The summers of 1968-69 were filled with trips to the beach, swimming, beer, cigarettes, and overnights with a litany of girlfriends. These escapades were interspersed with episodic bouts of depression and heart-wrenching guilt. But then summers also meant attending church camp where I could receive renewed forgiveness for my sins and return home refreshed and pure, prepped and ready to get it on again.

July 24: Well now I really prayed it all out and I really mean it!! I am serious this time and I'm going to try my hardest to stay this way. Sheri says she can go to the beach with me. If Robbie calls, I'll tell him I've changed.

CHURCH CAMP

Church Camp was at Jennings Lodge near Gladstone Oregon. Although it was held in the hottest week of July, girls were not allowed to wear shorts or sleeveless tops. Days were filled with Bible classes and singing and each night a huge meeting was held in an open-sided tabernacle. A prominent evangelist preached each evening and we would listen in anticipation for Friday night when we knew the preacher would implore the congregation to "get right with God". He would dare us to leave the service without doing so ("you might walk out of this place and be killed in a car wreck before Jesus can save your soul").

Thousands of congregants would join together in harmony to sing "Just As I Am Without A Plea", a plaintive confessional hymn describing all humans as inherently sinful pieces of shit who, but for the Grace of Jesus, are destined to aimlessly wander down the dark passages of life, directly into the arms of the devil. By the end of the second verse, a few brave souls would have made their way to the altar in front of the stage to kneel, sobbing for forgiveness. A few more folks would join them after the third verse but (wait for it!) by the end of the fourth and last verse, almost every person in the building had come to the altar. Sobbing and piercing prayers filled the air and we were all filled with the joy and relief of knowing that, at least that night, we weren't going to hell.

The summer of 1968 I met Greg at church camp. He was about my age, slightly built with blond hair, and unusually pale. One day during free time, we began to amble together around the perimeter of the camp. We chatted for a while and then he said, "I need to tell you something. It's something I have never told anyone. Ever. Can you keep a secret?" I assured him I could. "I'm gay" he said. I was befuddled. I knew that gay = homosexuality = sin = Hell. I was familiar with the Bible stories about Sodom and Gomorrah, but Greg was just a sweet young teenage boy attending church camp. I didn't know what to say so I said nothing. Not one word. We returned to camp in silence and never spoke to one another again.

Later than week, I was sitting with a young man at one of the tabernacle services. Before the beginning of the service we had struck up a conversation and he told me he was there for the evening with his parents. As the closing hymn began, the congregation was asked to stand up if they "felt the holy spirit", so, of course, I stood up. Then we were instructed to "lift our hands to God". I obeyed without hesitation and noticed that my new friend was still sitting in the pew staring at his shoes. I quietly asked him why he wasn't standing up. What was wrong? He looked me in the eye, and he replied, "I wish it was that simple". I knew he was right. Something didn't ring true with all of this emotional blubbering and urgency.

My sanctification was short-lived....

August 30: I'm staying with Debra. We went to Elwood's party for Esten up East Mapleton Road. It was a booze party and I got smashed. It was a mistake. I'm sorry I did it.

BACK TO SCHOOL

I returned to school for my Junior year and threw myself into the usual busyness. I had resumed kneeling by my bed every night and praying for forgiveness, even though I wasn't sure if God had any more patience with me.

November 12: Taught Junior Choir after school, went to an Honor Society Meeting. Gave Marilyn her piano lesson. I played "The Holy City" on my baritone accompanied by the band. Then I went to play practice.

December 10: The music concert was tonight. I sang, played piano, baritone, and violin.

I had a variety of boyfriends but that's what they were: friends. It was somewhat of a status symbol to have a boyfriend. My journals are filled with the drama of "getting" a new boyfriend, breaking up, and the angst of wanting a boyfriend. I swore never to fall in love again.

1969

January 22: I got my license!

January 23: I got a speeding ticket today! I was so shocked! I cried. Paula Findlay was with me. She's staying with me tonight. It was just terrible! Mom and Dad and Larry were wonderful about it. I have to go to court just like a convict.

I learned years later that Larry didn't feel that "wonderful" about my speeding ticket. In fact, he harbored deep resentment because I had not received any punishment. Dad had told Larry when he obtained his license that if Larry got a speeding ticket, his driving privileges would be suspended. But instead of being angry my father said, "It's easy to drive too fast on that stretch of road".

Over time, Larry became increasingly surly and rude. Dinner could become particularly contentious and, after his outbursts I would try to comfort my parents by saying "he didn't really mean that". At times he would lash out at me and Mom would say "Larry, don't talk that way to your sister!"

February 12: Jerry Rarick was killed in a two-car crash today. I had to do the write-up for the paper. It was simply awful. The high school looked like a morgue with a bunch of zombies roaming the halls. Larry and Mr. Ellis lowered the flag to half-mast and we had an assembly. I gave Marilyn her piano lesson.

February 27: I gave Faith her piano lesson. Cleaned popcorn machine with Don then he brought me home. I fixed a casserole. I took Aunt Emma's car down to get a head light bulb put in. Brought it home, left it in neutral and it started to roll down the hill. So I ran after it, jumped in, and smashed my head on the side of the car. But the car's fine.

May 23: Had a ball tonight. Peg, Lorene and I went to the (Rhododendron) Carnival. Then these guys were following us, so they followed us up South Jetty road. They were three college guys. They talked us into coming to their "camp" which was really a fire on the beach. I got drunk. Had a royal blast!

I failed to let my parents (who were not home when I left) know I was going to the Carnival in Florence. It was a school night which meant I would be home at least by 10:00 P.M. Dad was backing the car out of the driveway as Peggy drove me up to our house at 3:00 A.M. Neither Dad nor I spoke as I went to bed. I awoke in the morning and realized in a panic that I needed to fabricate some plausible explanation before we all sat down together for breakfast. Everyone was quiet as we sat down, and I began to explain how I had been helping Peggy with her car or something when Mom interrupted me and said, "I don't want to hear anything from you right now because I know it will be a lie. You are grounded for a month". I was more upset that I had lost her trust than I was about being grounded. I was only allowed to get in a car with Arta Lynn Upton (one of the "good" girls) for the next few months because that's the only way my Mom knew I would be safe (not get into trouble).

THE ARGUMENT

Larry graduated from high school in May of 1969. He was dating Jane Anderson, the daughter of a construction company owner in town. Larry was often gone, either working or spending time at her home. One day I began to leave for some sort of activity with friends and Mom said I could use the family car. But Larry said he needed the car for a date with Jane. He screamed saying that it was his right to use the car - that he was older and more important than me. I replied that he may as well change his name to "Anderson" because he was acting more like he belonged to the Anderson family than the Martin family. His face turned red as he told me to say I was sorry, to get on my knees, and ask for forgiveness.

With one swift motion I swept the books, magazines and knickknacks off the coffee table onto the floor. I could hear the tinkle of glass as I charged out of the door. My brother found me thirty minutes later, still seething, sitting on a log in my favorite spot in the woods overlooking the Siuslaw Valley. He apologized and I probably forgave him, but things were never the same between us after that.

LET'S PARTY!

I continued to attend church, pray for forgiveness, teach Sunday School, and go to alcohol-fueled parties up East Mapleton Road. When my cousin visited from La Grande, I sucked her into my pathological self-destructive spiral into hell.

July 11: Cousin Barb is visiting for a few weeks! She, Deb S and I went to the Drive-in. We took Deb home and went to Elwood's house. We stayed till 4:30 A.M. Barb and I got drunk. Barb's first time. Drove home like that. Barfed twice. Uncle Don and Aunt Pat are here.

That summer I rode a Greyhound Bus to visit my wealthy uncle (mom's brother) in Colorado. Uncle Calvin owned uranium mines, Appaloosa horses, and lived on a rambling ranch in the country. His youngest son Chris, named after our Great Uncle Chris Schneider, owned a new red Mustang and enjoyed shooting guns, going to stock car races, taking drugs and partying with a cadre of long-haired boys and scantily clad girls.

June 26: Aunt Emma and I got to Grand Junction at 1:00 A.M. after riding all day on the bus! We got to their house by 4:00 A.M.

June 27: Cousin Chris is a cool head. They smoke pot and drop pills here. Everything's cool. I went to the drive-in with Chris and his friend where I commenced to get drunk.

We smoked cigarettes, pot, and consumed alcohol during the week of my stay. I haven't seen Chris since then. I think he ended up somewhere in Hawaii. I apparently made it home safely with no arrests during that stay.

July 20: Neil Armstrong walked on the moon today! The United States has done it! Susan and I went swimming at Rain Rock. Deb Skinner is leaving tomorrow for Texas for good so Deb L and I had a slumber party. We had a séance and got Kathy C's grandmother!

We had seances, made out with our boyfriends, and played music on my portable 45 record-player in the sand dunes. One hot summer day in July, Deb Lindsey and I floated three miles on an inner tube down the Siuslaw from Brickerville to Mapleton with a 6-pack of beer. It was dark by the time we climbed onto the city dock and made our way to the grocery store, dripping wet, to call our parents for a ride. We did not get in trouble. All in all, my parents were appropriately attentive and encouraged my independence.

Larry left for school at Pacific College in Forest Grove in the Fall and I began my senior year of high school.

PART II: THE DIARIES

1969 - 1973

ONLY CHILD

I remained very busy my senior year of high school. I taught piano lessons, directed a weekly Junior Choir at the church, danced in the drill team, played girls hockey, acted in plays, was editor of the school yearbook, accompanied school choir as a pianist, and played in the pep band at every home game (basketball and football) and more. Fortunately, Mapleton was a small town. The school was a five-minute drive from our house, so it was possible (and even usual) to participate in several activities after school without spending hours in the car or on a bus. Entries in my diaries document getting home after ten or eleven at night and doing homework well after midnight. My grades were consistently good, and my life was full and rewarding. It was a good life.

September 25, 1969: I went to Dr. Myers today for my headaches. All he could say about my head was that I was crazy. And then I lost my contact at the A & W.

(Really?)

This was the first time I had been told that something may be wrong with my mind. I doubt that medical doctors knew very much about mental illness in 1969. But I am appalled that a medical professional would tell a teenage girl she was "crazy".

I spent countless hours with friends. Our gang of girls went to the beach where we sat around the campfire late into the night, went to drive-in movies (but did we ever really watch them?), and stayed overnight with one another. During school, Don Beck and I copied Rod McKuen poems and passed them to each other during class. He and I were good friends, although he often took advantage of my naivety. We once tromped through a pasture late at night, into the woods so he could show me an old Indian burial ground. It was only a big pile of sticks, but I believed him.

1970

January 23: I went to the doctor because I feel so tired. I don't have Mono. He says I'm just nervous.

Walter Cronkite continued to report news about the Vietnam War and the related plethora of anti-war protest marches. Throngs of college students and teenagers marched the streets of Chicago, Washington D.C., and New York carrying signs about stopping the war and the promoting of peace. I watched as the boys burned their draft cards and continued to watch as they were handcuffed by police and thrown into vans. And I watched in what seemed to be slow motion as the Ohio National Guard fired 67 rounds into a crowd of unarmed students at Kent State on May 4th killing four students and wounding nine others.

UNEXPECTED NEWS

On May 18th, Larry and Jane, who were by then engaged to be married, came home from college. It was my father's 50th birthday and I thought it was very nice of them to take time out of their busy college schedules to attend his birthday celebration. After the candles had been blown out and we had eaten cake and ice cream, Larry asked if I could excuse myself, because he and Jane wanted to have some time alone with Mom and Dad.

I drove to a friend's house for a visit and thought nothing more about it. The next day was a Saturday and, although the weather hadn't turned particularly warm, Mother was lying on a blanket on the front yard. She was crying but wouldn't tell me what was wrong. Dad was seated in his recliner staring into space. Larry asked me to go for a drive and we drove to the church and parked. Jane was pregnant.

Well, that put a monkey wrench in the works!

Jane's family was quite disapproving and even hostile. They had promised to provide a honeymoon trip to Hawaii to Larry and Jane for a wedding gift, but instead gave them a frying pan. Not an electric frying pan. Just a frying pan. They now required Jane to ring their doorbell, and she had to request permission to visit.

My father addressed our graduating class of 1970 and appeared to be uncharacteristically sad and reserved as he talked about our responsibility to make a difference in the world. At the conclusion of the graduation ceremony Jane and Larry left for Reno to get married. A few days later Dad informed me that he had accepted a position as superintendent of schools for the Neahkahnie School District in Rockaway. We were moving.

I believe that my parents were painfully embarrassed because of Larry and Jane's unplanned pregnancy and felt that they had to move to another school district in order to make a fresh start. Her parents thought that Larry should drop out of school and work in the woods, but my parents were adamant that he should continue his education and they paid for the remainder of his schooling. Larry and Jane lived with us for the next few months until they moved to Corvallis where Larry would attend OSU.

I did not have any stress or concern about college plans. My father was an Oregon State University Alumni. No other plans were discussed about my options for the future. We were Beavers so, OSU it was.

My Scholastic Aptitude Test (S.A.T.) score was initially the highest in our class but Dianna Gordon, my academic nemesis, complained that because she had dental work just prior to taking the exam, she should be allowed to take it again. Mr. Pambren, the Social Studies teacher and S.A.T. test proctor, was particularly fond of Dianna and allowed her to retake the exam. She scored a few points higher than me. I casually applied to attend OSU and was promptly accepted. There was no interview and no invitation to tour the campus. I didn't have any professional or academic goal, but I was going to college.

The Mapleton Covered Bridge was demolished one month after we moved.

TOO YOUNG

September 8: The Arab terrorists have approximately 100 American hostages held in Israel. Could get very sticky.

My father drove me to Corvallis during the second week of September. He parked the car in front of McNary Hall and opened the trunk of our 1969 Chevy Impala and handed me two suitcases. I hugged him "goodbye" and I turned to walk towards the dormitory while he drove away. I checked in at the front desk and was handed a key for my room on the second floor. I stepped into the elevator and was greeted by a bubbly red-headed girl loaded down with suitcases and boxes. She smiled broadly and said "Hi! My name is Gail". I opened the door of room 214 and met my roommate Kathy, a dour surly young woman who most certainly suffered from some sort of mood and/or personality disorder. She was gone by October and bubbly Gail Ragsdale from Cave Junction moved in with me.

On the evening of that first day, the girls on our floor were told to attend a mandatory resident meeting. The RA (Resident Assistant) asked us to introduce ourselves and state our major area of study. I suddenly realized that I had not decided what the focus of my study would be, or even which classes to take. I said that I would be majoring in Education.

McNary Hall had been designated as the first coed residence at Oregon State University, and for the first time, members of the opposite sex would reside in the same building. The floors were gender-specific, but the only thing keeping us apart was the stairwell and the elevator. Rules banning the intermingling of boys and girls between 10:00 PM and 6:00 AM were strictly enforced for a few weeks, but eventually all efforts to keep the sexes apart were abandoned.

I would love to tell you that I excelled in school but, unfortunately, that first year of college was a fiasco. My parents were footing the bill, and, at seventeen years of age, I was too immature to be left alone to my own devices at a huge state university campus. I soon realized that no one cared if I attended classes and, for the first time in my life I was anonymous. I met with an inept advisor to review my class schedule and she signed off on my desire to take an upper division Shakespeare class as an elective.

September 20: I am at O.S.U. My roommate's name is Kathy Smith. Have another good friend – Gail. So far so good. No hang-ups.

September 30: 8:00 Lit. Then went to advisor and picked up geography and hockey. Too busy. So that will give me 16 hours. I feel very nostalgic for some reason. College is where I belong. I love it. It's work. I smoked the last weed of my life today. Bleck!

October 5: 8:00 Lit. Still reading "The Gesture". 1:00 Math – I skipped. 3:00 Geography – left half-way through. I slept, studied a little. Feel sick kind of. Kathy's gone. Gail is staying with me.

October 26: I flunked my geography test. Flat out. I want to quit the dumb class. Good idea. Almost finished with my history paper. I have to Xerox a bunch of stuff, but it's written. The wind was cold – beautiful – I love it!

November 5: I didn't go to any classes today. Slept till about 11:00. Felt so good. Went to town with Jeannie and Gail. Got some $27 boots.

December 17: I'm home! Yay! Took Shakespeare test at 2:00. I got up and studied till 12:00 then till 1:00 after lunch. I have no idea whatsoever as to how I did. None. Possible "F". Very possible! Packed, said goodbyes. Daddy came at 7:00 to pick me up.

I was home for Christmas break when the grades arrived in the mail. I flunked the Shakespeare class.

I returned to school after Christmas break and found that some of my friends had become quite somber. Their grades had also been bad, and they were on the brink of losing financial support from their parents. They no longer wanted to stay up late into the night talking and goofing around. But my poor grades had not deterred me one bit.

1971

January 17: Larry called at 3:00 this morning to say Jane was going to the Hospital. I got up at 7:00 and Jesse walked over there with me. Gail came trotting in minutes after. It's a boy! Larry Gordon Martin! (original name) Mom and Dad came over and just missed it. What an experience. What a beautiful baby!

February 5: This night has been unbelievable. Dave called and asked me out for the wrestling meet. We went, then tripped over to his apartment. Then over here. He stayed overnight. I couldn't believe myself. Oh God.

February 6: Went to Dave's and watched the OSU – OREGON basketball game. Then went over to Larry's and saw Mother and Father. Then we went to a Kegger at Campus Villa.

February 7: I slept in until 12:30. I felt awful all day. Smoking cigarettes and drinking Cold Duck. Really dumb. Thought a lot. Mainly about God and me – our relationship and how it should be.

February 13: Up at 11:00. Went to bookstore. Sat around all day. Dave picked me up at 6:30. We went to "Thunderball" then went to his apartment and had vodka and orange juice and pizza.

February 18: I am so screwed up right now. I love God but my willpower is zilch, and I am uncertain as to what I really should do with my life. It's such a big empty hole right now and I have no one but myself to blame.

I wrote the following song and can still sing it today with my guitar:

April 20:   *Alone can be lonely when I'm in my room*
                By myself.
                Can be lonely, thinking of a friend and the years left behind.
                Love was here, now has gone away
                Can be lonely when I'm all alone.
                Tears can be lonely when they're over you
                Over me.

                Once a friend, with a smile
                With a hand to hold.
                Once you cared
                Once you dared,
                Once you shared for me
                Without you
                Can be lonely too.

                Loving can be lonely. Love's for two,
                Yours has left and gone.
                Feel so helpless
                What I said? What I didn't do?

                Can't you see?
                I am me
                And I'll always be loving you my friend
                Till the end

I continued to sleep in, skip class, and attend parties. Gail was in
love with David who lived on the next floor. "Our" room became
the hang-out for our friends. One evening David sat with me in the
student lounge and, as an atheist, articulately explained away the
existence of God. My head was spinning with the notions of NO
GOD = NO SIN = NO GUILT. I was in a blur, felt detached from
reality, and felt ill the next morning. I was returning to my dorm
from Introductory to English where I had spent the previous hour in

a daze and spoke aloud to God. I apologized for doubting His existence and suddenly I felt better, but I continued to be depressed with a great deal of angst and guilt. I was certain that my life was meaningless and that I was a lost cause. I had simply sinned too much.

On May 30th I was making out with Stan Schmokel (an older student who furnished a steady flow of alcohol), when his knee hit my kneecap causing it to dislodge to the side of my leg. He ran to find my friend Casey, who without hesitation, popped the kneecap back into place. I screamed in pain and she gave me two pills (who knows what they were?!). I awoke lying on a bed in the school infirmary with ice on my knee. I was placed in an ankle to hip plaster cast and finished finals week walking with crutches.

May 30: Stan stayed all night. This morning he rolled over on me and knocked my kneecap off. Really cute. Really hurt. We went to the infirmary accompanied by Casey. They're keeping me for a while. Kathy and Stan and Casey and Mike all came over to see me. It's really not too bad. A lot of attention.

I had never been a very good liar and told my mom that some books had fallen on my knee.

My grade point for the year was 2.5 and I knew I could not return to OSU the following year. If I did I would surly dissolve into nothing.

June 10: I'm through and home.

A FRESH START

My parents had moved to a large old beach home in Rockaway on a ridge looking out over the ocean. Dad was now Superintendent of Schools for the Neahkahnie School District. I worked in the summer at a local drive-in hamburger joint where I earned $1.25 an hour and spent my free time walking on the beach with my dog Soxy.

June 16:   I watched him today
*   Strolling through the park. Slowly.*

Occasionally pausing to look at the ground or his feet.
I don't know.
Then gazing across the grass at the trees, up to the clouds, down
again.
Thinking. Heavy. I could feel it.
Wondering about God. I knew that's what it was.
Maybe questioning, perhaps saddened by his own disbelief.
What to believe in? I felt it too.

I knew I couldn't return to OSU in the Fall. One day as I walked barefoot on the beach in the wet sand, I wondered if the world would be better off without me. I was certain that I was too weak, that I lacked the self-control necessary to live a sinless life and began to contemplate the advantage of just walking straight into the ocean westward into the depths of the sea. I stopped and stared into the horizon where the sun had begun to set, and I began to cry. I hadn't cried for many months. I felt numb, stupid, and hopeless.

I still had no inkling about where I wanted to go with my life, no wisp of a thought that maybe, someday, I could achieve any academic or professional goals. I needed to be protected from the evil sirens waiting to drag me into hell. I remembered that I had once accompanied Diana McCaslin when she visited George Fox College, a small Christian school in Newberg, Oregon. George Fox had rules, lots of rules. I would be safe there.

I majored in Christian Education and minored in Music at George Fox College and carried 21 credits a term (12 credits a term was considered full time). I took Music theory, Orchestra, Choir, Bible and Christian Education classes and private violin lessons from a greasy-haired unkempt older gentleman. I was, for the first time in so very long, hopeful that I could learn to live a chaste life, but I still had no specific goal.

After I read a book required for of my Christian Education classes, I began to conceptualize God as a bit less fickle and vindictive. "Love Is Now", by Peter Gilquist, described a God of Love. I read about how God wants the best for us, and that, as a loving Father, He feels our pain. I began to believe that perhaps God wasn't just sitting up in heaven waiting for me to sin so He could send me to Hell.

Although I was attending a Christian college, it turned out that I was not entirely protected from the temptations of the world. One evening, my friend Sharon Murphy ("Murph") and I took a walk, maybe to go buy a milkshake at the Dairy Queen. It was about 9:00 PM as we headed back towards campus, and we could hear loud music blaring from the (off-campus) house where most of the George Fox soccer team lived. Most of the team were from South America, Peru I think, and, for some reason, the foreign students were allowed to live off campus in their own house. As we passed their house, Murph recognized one of the young men, and he invited us in for a visit. A drink was placed in my hand as soon as we stepped in the door, and we joined a small crowd of Spanish-speaking young men as they sang, danced, and drank a variety of adult beverages. The next thing I remember is Murph grabbing my arm, insisting that we needed to leave. We had apparently been there for several hours and I was nicely inebriated. Guilt, of course, washed over me as we stumbled back to the dorm and I awoke the next day with a dreadful hangover and the certainty that I just too weak, too damaged to live a sinless life. What kind of person could attend a Christian College where there were strict rules against drinking, and still manage to stumble into an alcohol-infused party? I told no one about our escapade and to this day Murph and I share this naughty little secret. Well, until now.

I was privileged to join a female quartet while at George Fox and loved the beauty and energy of joining our voices together as we sang in close harmony while playing a variety of instruments. Shelly played the tambourine, Divonna played the violin and flute, Patty played the piano, and I played the guitar and violin as we sang together about God's love. We travelled around the Northwest singing for churches and conferences and often ended performance days eating dinner together at a restaurant. One night we were at Denny's in East Portland and a group of men dressed as women walked past our table. Shelley said, "It looks like there are some gay guys eating here tonight". Divonna laughed and agreed that they did indeed look gay since they were dressed up like women. I asked her if she knew what being "gay" meant, and she said, "oh they're just very happy". Shelley whispered into Divonna's ear that "gay" was a term used to describe men who were sexually attracted to other men. Divonna's face turned white, she jumped up from the table, and ran to the bathroom to vomit. She had been raised in a sheltered Christian home and her only understanding of homosexuality was that it was the worst of all sins. She was totally unaware that a significant number of our society had begun to identify as "gay".

Our quartet performed for the spring concert at George Fox College in June, and my parents were in attendance, seated towards the back of the auditorium. We performed beautifully and after the concert, as I headed up the aisle to join my parents, I could see that Mom was quite upset. With tears streaming down her cheeks she said, "I hate to tell you this Honey, but Shelley is pregnant". I laughed because Shelley was a clean-cut Christian girl from St. Helens. She had no boyfriend that I knew of and, anyway, as a good Christian, she couldn't possibly be pregnant. Two weeks later Shelley suddenly disappeared from campus. She reconnected with me one year later to tell me that she had become pregnant with a young man she had met in town and after seeking guidance from the George Fox chaplain, she had been advised to get an abortion which she described as a "freeing" experience. This was in a different era and abortion had not yet become a divisive topic among Christians. When I attended George Fox, abortion was still considered to be a reasonable solution for an unwanted pregnancy, even by college chaplains.

I met Ron Hays in December 1971. He was kind, funny, sweet, and had a passion for social justice. Like me, he was a child of educators; however, he had been raised in the Quaker faith. He was very good looking. We began dating around February 1972, although by then he had dropped out of school to help care for his mother who was dying from cancer.

1972

I returned to Rockaway to my parent's home at the end of Spring Term. I had achieved a 4.00 grade point average, but Dad could see that I lacked direction and, more importantly, he was skeptical of the quality and content of the education I had received at George Fox. In addition, it was much more expensive than a state school. He asked his school guidance counselor Mr. Gilbertson to give me an aptitude test to evaluate which profession I would be best suited for and the number one professional fit for me was "psychologist". The second-best fit was "nurse". I loved the notion of becoming a psychologist. Human behavior was fascinating! But I was obviously not smart enough to be a psychologist. I decided to become a nurse.

Unfortunately for Ron, the Vietnam War draft had caught up with him. The whole military draft was a socio-economic travesty. Simply put, if you had money to attend college, you couldn't be drafted but If you were poor and couldn't afford to attend college, you would probably be drafted. Ron had dropped out of school to help care for his ailing mother and, regardless of his very good reason for not being in school, he was drafted. He was a Quaker which meant that, as a pacifist, he could not be forced to serve in the military. He was instead required to serve two years of "alternate service" which meant that he could work for a non-profit organization if approved by his draft board. An old friend of his family was working at a facility for Juvenile Delinquent boys in Alaska and Ron was given permission to work there.

I broke up with him when he visited me in Rockaway in early June, one week before he left for Alaska. I knew I didn't love him, not as a wife should love a husband. And I did feel very badly about it because Ron knew he would never see his mother again when he left Oregon to work at Turning Point Boys Ranch as a counselor. She died on August 17th.

September 6: Today eleven Olympic Jewish athletes were killed. Probably very honest young men, guys I would probably look at a second time. Young men with healthy strong bodies and most likely healthy young minds, willing minds. They meant to hurt no one. They were representing their country which just happened to be Israel. It's hard to hold back the bitterness I feel. I hold a high place and respect for innocence. It is quite an attribute, yet one cannot call it an attribute because innocence is not attained. It does not result from maturity. It just is. And the eleven were innocent.

The Arabs were wrong, though the "Black Septembers" represent only a very small portion of the Arab government. Yet they must be held responsible and face the consequences since they were not willing to help West Germany negotiate. It is a shame. I am bitterly confused. Isn't there something that we, the youth of today, can do to help? Help What? To help prevent or help stall the nuclear war that is sure to come. To knock some sense into a few people's heads. I feel helpless. I am caught in today's wars, famines, and poverty and I can either close my eyes and pretend they aren't there, or I can open my eyes and willingly take on the mess of today. But how? In what manner? With what skills, with what objectives? Help us Lord!

ANOTHER COLLEGE

I began my third year of college at University of Oregon in September 1972 where I enrolled in the pre-nursing program. I was intellectually invigorated by the Chemistry, Biology, Nutrition, and Psychology classes required for admission to the School of Nursing and had easily earned straight A's by the end of Fall term.

November 26: I wish I could someday write a book about life and say to future generations "Take it. Read it. Don't make the same mistakes I did.

Memorize these rules I have devised for living a good life". Actually, someday I do plan on writing a book. It will be about God's love in my life. It's the only thing worth writing about.

The director of the nursing program stood before the pre-nursing class in a cavernous lecture hall at the end of Fall term and said "If any of you are not 100% sure that you want to be a nurse, get out of my program now!". I was shaken and felt dizzy. I had never seen blood or wounds or urine. I didn't know if I could be a nurse: In hindsight, the director asked if we *wanted* to be nurses, not whether we *could* be nurses.

What to do? In a panic I hurried to the registrar's office to change my major to "Education" (always a good fallback plan). Ron continued to write several letters a week and I began to warm to the idea of having a serious relationship with him.

December 9: Ron, I don't want to hurt you so, I hope, I really hope that I love you. I want to love you. You are the man I've always looked for. You have all the attributes I've ever looked for in a husband. I would be so very proud to marry you. So, I hope that I love you. If I do, we belong together. Forever.

1973

January 1: I am probably in love with him and am anxious to find out. The future looks so bright yet uncertain.

January 8: I just wrote to Ron. I am afraid that I don't love him because I really want to love him! I want it to work out for us. I'm praying it will.

January 21: I admit that occasionally I doubt but then I doubt my salvation now and then too, deep down knowing what's right is right. Ron came tonight around 10:00. We are officially engaged!

Ron came home for a visit in January and asked me to marry him. By now I was taking a jumbled combination of elementary education classes and some electives. I had dropped all pretense of majoring in

Education by Spring Term and instead took psychology and sociology classes which, of course, I loved. I was impatient for the school year to end because now I had a wedding to plan.

January 23: We went home to tell Mother and Father. They were very happy and pleased with Ron. Dad got into this bit about was I going to finish my education but that was all. We told him we would finish. I hope he can trust us enough to use our own wisdom because I know he's worried that I won't finish school. We will though.

February 8: I am a different person. I am engaged. I am a woman. I love Ron, and he loves me. We will be together spiritually and mentally for as long as we both shall live. Hopefully we will be together physically as well. It is a wonderful feeling knowing that I have found him, the man of my dreams. It is too good to be true. It must be of God.

February 18: Swanee and I went to the Eugene Friends Church for both morning and evening services. I was extremely impressed. I am going to start attending, I think. I could really feel God's presence and the people are super friendly.

Ron was a Quaker and I was attracted to their doctrinal emphasis on social justice and peace. Don Lamm, pastor of the Eugene Friends (Quaker) Church, spoke of love and grace. There was no mention of hell or damnation and his sermons focused on how to live a Christ-like (Christian) life. I wrote daily in "The Kahil Gibran Diary for 1973" up until three days before my wedding. As the wedding drew closer the content becomes increasingly shallow and filled with the desperate hope that I will be able to love Ron enough. I do not recognize this person who wrote these superficial entries replete with "praise God" and "I love Ron". I was trying to convince myself that, because Ron had come into my life, I was redeemed, saved from a life of sin. Life would now be a stream of Jesus-infused joy.

I had begun to work at a sandwich shop in downtown Eugene the beginning of February. I was leaning over to wipe (bus) a table when suddenly a wave of pain shot through my back and down my legs. I crumpled into the seat of the booth and I sat there, frozen for several minutes. When I tried to stand the pain worsened, but I was determined to get back to work. I somehow finished my shift, mopping floors and cleaning counters. I collapsed into bed that night, unable to move. I was seen the next morning at the student health center and given muscle relaxers. The pain persisted for the following three months and, decades later, I would have two back surgeries.

I lived in a Christian Co-op during Winter and Spring terms. Ron's best friend Dan Swanson ("Swanee") moved in around the same time. We became very close and I loved him so much as a friend! We spent hours together taking walks, studying, staying up until the wee hours of the morning just visiting, and going to the beach. At the end of Spring Term, I flew to Alaska to visit Ron for a week so we could discuss wedding plans and get to know one another a bit better.

Swanee handed me an envelope before I left and asked that I wait until I was in the air before I read it. As the tires tucked under the plane, I began reading the letter. Swanee had written that he loved me more than just a friend; he wanted me to know that. However, as Ron's best friend, he knew that we could never be lovers. He was too good of a friend, too honorable to cross that line. A wave of doubt encompassed me as I wondered whether my love for Ron was really any different than the love that I felt for Swanee.

Ron came home a few days before the wedding. His great uncle Oscar Brown officiated but required that we meet for "counseling" before he would marry us. He admonished us to "never let the sun go down on your wrath" (Ephesians 4:26). We took this advice to heart. As a result, we occasionally argued well into the early morning for years to come. Our differences were usually "resolved" when I simply became weary and conceded to Ron's side of the argument.

A few days before my wedding in July, I realized that I did not know how to cook. I had taken choir and band instead of home-economics, and Mom hadn't even tried to teach me much about domestic skills. I told her that I didn't know how to cook, and she said, "can you read? There's my recipe box. Help yourself." As a result, to this day, my daughter's favorite meal is tater tot casserole.

We were married on July 28, 1973 at the Rockaway Community Church. As we drove away from the church to spend our first night as man and wife, I thought, "What have I done?". I did not write in a journal again for two years.

PART III: THE JOURNALS

1973 – 1984

NORTH TO ALASKA

We loaded up his 1965 Ford pickup two days after the wedding and began the 2,600-mile journey up the Alcan Highway, through Canada to Willow Alaska. Ron had purchased a used 60-foot mobile home situated at Turning Point Boys Ranch. This facility for juvenile delinquents was surrounded by a ring of various sizes and shapes of mobile homes belonging to the other staff, who, like us, were young adults. The men worked various shifts while the wives remained at home. Women were not allowed to walk into the complex, except for the director Eileen Hahn who ran the facility with an iron fist.

I was thrown into a routine of housework and cooking, shopping and visiting with the other wives. We were very poor: Ron made $300 a month, and, after the monthly mortgage, we had about $50 a month. We argued once in the grocery store aisle about whether we could afford to purchase chocolate chips. My parents visited for Christmas and Mom cried on the plane trip home because she was certain that I was destined to be stuck in the wilds of Alaska, barefoot and pregnant for the remainder of my life.

We lived about 70 miles North of Anchorage in the woods with dirt roads, snow and ice. Craggy mountains loomed in the distance and it was romantically beautiful. And lonely. By January, I was pregnant and fell into a deep pervasive depression. The twenty-four-hour darkness of winter fed my depression and I seldom got out of bed. As the days grew longer I began to feel the flutter of life within my womb, my emotional state improved, and I was ready to pack our things for a move back to Oregon when Ron completed his two-year commitment for Alternate Service in July. We moved to Corvallis where Ron attended OSU, and Jonathan Gordon Hays was born on September 12, 1974. I was twenty-one years old.

MOTHERHOOD

Ron had to stand in the corner of the delivery room wearing a mask, gown, and gloves when it was finally time for Jonathan to enter the world. The birthing experience was horrific. Ron could not initially accompany me to the labor room where I would remain for almost two days. The nurses were grumpy, I couldn't eat, and I felt like I was in a prison of pain. Ron was eventually allowed to join me in the labor room but only for a few minutes at a time. I had not prepared for childbirth. How hard could it be? Women had babies every day.

The first time I held Jonathan was the most joyful moment of my life. I was awash with euphoria and marveled that this small creature had been created by me. By us. I was so very happy! Ron was not allowed to touch or hold Jonathan until we were discharged to home.

Jonathan was a fussy and cranky baby and we were neurotic parents. I had studied behavioral psychology theory and believed that a baby was born as a "tabula rasa", literally a blank slate. Everything this child would become (his intelligence, his happiness, his personality) was dependent on his environment. The quality of our parenting would ultimately determine who this baby would become. I was terrified

We lived in an old small duplex apartment with mold growing in the closets. I had become friends with a woman who was a zealous member of the Le Leche League, an organization that promoted breast feeding, a practice not very prevalent in 1974. Research supported the physiological and psychological benefits of nursing and feeding an infant on demand, but this contradicted the pediatrician's instruction to breast feed no more than once every four hours and to let him scream and cry himself to sleep.

I began to recognize that, as a mother, I instinctually knew what was best for my baby. I spent the first six months of Jonathan's life holding, rocking, nursing, and learning to do housework with one hand because he was so irritable and fussy. Ron was as supportive as he could be while taking classes full time and working an evening job on campus. I was bewildered that other women would choose to have more than one baby. This was not fun or rewarding and I felt ugly and depressed.

Ron discovered in April that he had been poorly advised about class prerequisites and that he would not be able to complete his degree during the next year. We believed that God Himself had intervened when Ron received a phone call from the director of Turning Point Boys Ranch asking him to return as the assistant director. We made arrangements to purchase a small run-down trailer at the Ranch and headed back to Alaska.

1975

August 8: My, much has taken place since the last writing! I'm a mother. Just the sound of the word makes me feel older. No, make that more mature. It has changed me. It has changed Ron. This entire experience of parenthood has made us new people. Closer. Quieter. More patient. More content to be with each other, doing nothing in particular except playing with the little one who, I'm afraid is getting bigger every day. God has taught me much about myself, through Jonathan. There's so much I need to work on. The biggest is selfishness.

We attended a small community church where I occasionally played the piano and violin. Our home became a refuge for the unmarried staff at Turning Point Boy's Ranch. Jonathan was loved and surrounded by a family of "uncles' who would come for dinner and stay late into the night playing card games. As winter began and the days became short, I began to feel despondent and worthless. I did not believe that I deserved to be loved by Ron and, on more than one occasion, contemplated packing a suitcase and leaving. I believed that Jonathan and Ron would be better off if I just disappeared. I did not know what was wrong with me and had no idea that my symptoms were consistent with the diagnosis of Depression.

1976

April 3: Today I washed the walls.

    Cupboards with little fingerprints: chocolate fingerprints, gluey fingerprints, black-ink fingerprints.
    And little pen marks on the hallway walls.
    No, not mischievousness, not rebellious. Just experimenting.
    Touching, feeling-for-the-first-time
    "What's -in-this-drawer?" markings.
    Oh thank you God for little fingerprints.
    Jonathan is busy busy busy! I love him so much!

April 9: It's raining, not snowing. Melting down the mountains into my front yard world.

Sitting on the steps watching the baby-boy discover the world without worrying about frost bit fingers. I'm leaving the windows open, breathing the Spring air. Yes, this rain opens a new world and I can't wait for the memories to return, once again, to reality.

One April day while sitting on our front porch watching Jonathan play with sticks in the dirt, I had a moment of clarity. By then my daily routine consisted of cleaning, laundry, shopping, cooking, changing diapers, and visiting with my neighbor Jean over a cup of coffee. I realized this was not what I wanted to be when I grew up. Hadn't I, in my former life, written stories and plays? Didn't I have a love of learning? Didn't I want to BE someone?

That Summer the State of Alaska implemented a federally funded pilot program for the development of rural emergency medical services and, as a result, our community received an ambulance, emergency equipment, and uniforms. Ron and I took one of the first Emergency Medical Technician (EMT) trainings in the country and we joined the Willow Volunteer Ambulance crew. My passion for helping others was reawakened after my first medical emergency call. I knew that someday I would be a nurse.

Over time, Ron and I fell into a comfortable rhythm although my episodic depression fueled by guilt and resentment sometimes disturbed that rhythm. Ron was quick to compliment me and was loving and patient, yet understandably frustrated by my lack of passion for him. But most of the time the demands of motherhood distracted me from the existential task of pondering meaning and purpose in life.

1977

January 18: I am resolved to reach my potential and to overflow it. It seems I've been just drifting within myself. Now I'm going to begin growing. Throwing aside fears and believing in a beautiful combination of God and me.

Ron was becoming dissatisfied with his job at Turning Point Boys Ranch, and, in the Spring, we began to talk about what we wanted to do with our lives. Mostly, we talked about the need for Ron to complete his college education and decided that Ron should return to George Fox College.

September 2: I ate at Willow Inn with Alvera and Jean today. Then we did the hardest thing – the "goodbyes". I fell apart with Jean. I was very sad to leave her. We met up with Jim and Nancy in Wasilla and went on to Sutton to camp.

We headed back down the Alcan Highway in September driving an old Ford Pickup from Willow Alaska to Newberg Oregon. Jonathan was twenty months old and sat on a booster seat between us. None of us wore seatbelts. We found a small ramshackle house in Newberg which had once been a chicken coop and lived there rent-free in exchange for labor: the owner provided supplies while Ron did the carpentry work necessary to maintain the home. We had a roof over our heads but living in that house turned out to be quite the adventure. One morning we awoke to find our bed surrounded by water from heavy rains. We had used up most of our money on moving and college expense, so I began to search for work.

Jonathan continued to be unpredictably cranky and would scream and wail when left with babysitters. One day I left him at a day care center for a few hours while I interviewed for some waitress jobs. When I returned, the caregiver met me at the door holding Jonathan. He had screamed for the entire three hours. He was shaking, his face was red, and streaks of red from broken blood vessels dotted his neck. I took Jonathan and, while he sobbed on my shoulder, handed her my last three dollars. I would not be working outside of the home.

1978

February 7: I have been babysitting since about November and cleaning house for the same lady. Ron's fall term went well. He got a 3.25 with 16 hours. Now he's working full time at the hospital on the ambulance and in the Emergency Room.

I taught piano lessons, babysat an out-of-control three-year-old, and cleaned house for his parents. Ron attended school and attended advanced EMT training and, through a series of fortunate events, was invited to apply for the Ambulance Department Supervisor position at Tillamook County General Hospital.

April 26: I want to leave....but I don't. Tillamook, of all places! But of utmost importance is Ron's contentment with his job.

I was seven months pregnant when we moved to Tillamook in June.

TILLAMOOK

August 16: I had a doctor's appointment this morning. Dr. Shawler said it* could come any time now because it's all in position, ready to come. Sometimes I feel so alone, what with Ron gone so much. I feel completely alone. Sometimes it turns into loneliness. Especially when I don't feel real well. I'm so thankful to have Jonathan to keep me active, and Jesus to talk to. I've got to learn to confide more in Him. After all, He wants to be my best friend if I'll only let Him.

*It: We never knew the gender of our babies before they were born.

Beth Michelle Hays was born on September 8, four days before her brother's 4th birthday. I had taken Lamaze classes and this time I was prepared for the physical and emotional demands of childbirth. When she entered the world, Dr. Shawler handed her to me, still gooey and wet. I greeted her with a happy heart. She was the most beautiful human being I had ever seen! Soon after her birth we began attending Netarts Friends Church.

1979

January 18: Tillamook has become "home" and, even though there are other more picturesque and suitable places to live in the world, we have and are still making some wonderful friends here. We are also becoming extremely active in community and church. I do thank the Lord for sending us here.

January 20: I can see why babies are called "bundles of love", "gifts from heaven", etc. Beth just shines with love. She has brought us so much joy!

January 27: My children are like precious jewels, irreplaceable for their unique beauty and sparkle. The joy they have brought me brings a new dimension to living. I'm drunk with the love that flows between us, when wet lips kiss me goodnight, when a little hand grasps mine for security, when eyes light up at the prospect of merely being held. The twinkle of innocence will remain in my memory long after it has been replaced by the solemnness of knowledge, and it is a memory that I, like all mothers throughout all time, will always cherish.

Life was full of diapers, breast-feeding, preschool for Jonathan, and long walks with Beth in the stroller. We were able to buy a new three-bedroom house with a house payment of $150 a month the following summer because we qualified for a low-income FHA housing loan. I had little time for existential or spiritual reflection. Ron was gone two to three days at a time due to his work schedule and I enjoyed providing a hospitable home for a variety of work and church-related friends. I played piano for church and soon stepped into the role of choir director. But something was still missing.

I decided to take a creative writing class when Beth was four months old. I needed to see what it felt like to attend a college class, to see whether I was still capable of learning. I sat in the back of the classroom breastfeeding Beth as I discovered that I had, indeed, retained the capacity for critical thinking and intellectual discourse.

1980

March 6: As I sit here waiting for Ron to come home while the television rambles along, I'm overcome with contentment, sad though it is. Yes, a Sad contentment. Oh, I'm so lonely and feel so unexciting. I live a bland lifestyle now, not doing what I would normally be doing simply because of a lack of emotional energy. My house is clean, my children are happy, and my husband is pleased that I'm staying home taking care of myself as well as them. We've money problems galore. Poor Ron. I must not pressure him with this. I must keep it to myself and its up to me to somehow stretch $60 through the month. The Lord is faithful, and He can do.

I called my brother on April 21ˢᵗ just to tell him "happy birthday". We had not spoken for years and it was his 30ᵗʰ birthday. He said, "We have nothing in common besides our blood. I don't really see any reason to have any more contact from now on." I was devastated. A month later I developed a serious infection and was hospitalized for three weeks. I suspect that this may have been some sort of psychosomatic response to the emotional trauma of being rejected by my only sibling.

Mom and Dad had moved to Mill City where Dad was superintendent of schools and Mom taught seventh grade. On May 18ᵗʰ we were standing in their back yard for Dad's 60ᵗʰ birthday party with dozens of friends and family who had come to celebrate his birthday when the ground shook and Mt. St. Helen's blew her top. During the party, Mom received a phone call from Jane. They would not be attending the party because they were putting a lawn in. As

Mom relayed the message to Dad, his face crumbled, and I was reminded of those times when Larry refused to go fishing with him.

I was sitting on the end of our bed on November 4th crying softly when six-year-old Jonathan walked into the bedroom and asked, "what's wrong Mom?" I explained to him that our very nice president Jimmy Carter had just been voted out of office and that another man Mr. Reagan, had been elected to be our next president. Jonathan snuggled up next to me, saying, "then I'm sad too" and we sat together for a while consoling one another. I would be very sad, once again, after another presidential election many years later.

1981

July 29: Married 8 years. 8. Years. How can it be? It seems that a dream has been in progress, much of it a blur, much of it clear and precise. Conversations lost in the wind, though retained in parts dissected in the mind, contorted and arranged to conform to current opinion. We continue to live on, comfortable with each other, hoping and believing that maybe the other one will supply all the answers, all the strength. Believing in each other. In us. Not much excitement really. No surprises, but once in a while a tender moment will cast a new glow, give us fresh air. I'm realizing that what must be done must be done. My mouth moves, spewing forth wishes, desires, plans, but what comes of it? I will pray for strength tonight. What is my driving force?

I began taking anatomy, chemistry, and microbiology classes at Tillamook Community College in the Fall of 1981 with plans to obtain a nursing degree. I was accepted to the Portland Community College School of Nursing the following year and began commuting to Portland for classes and clinical rotations in the Fall of 1982. We were very fortunate that Ron's sister Terry had moved to Tillamook and lived less than a block away so that I never had to worry about whether my children were well cared for in my absence.

Journals from 1981 – 1983 are missing. Either life was too busy to write during that period of my life or they were lost along the way.

1984

FINALLY, A NURSE

January 9: My nine-year-old son has just left on his bike (in a hurry as usual) for school. His parting words, so innocent and certainly not meant to hurt, pierced my heart. "I sure wish you didn't have to leave for school or even go to school! I'll sure be glad when it's over. I'm sure going to miss you. Bye. I love you!" I'd like to think that when I'm gone no one really misses me, that the void is immediately filled by their father and other important people, that they will not suffer in any way by my absence. I see the laundry baskets, filled to the brim spilling out all over the family room. Beds are unmade, dishes in the sink, the broom sits unused in the corner. That kind of neglect I can handle. But my children, so precious. Beth knows I'm going today, leaving for school. I've told her I'll be gone a while this time and she wrongly must assume that she'll see me tomorrow or maybe the next day. I don't know what she thinks. But she trusts me to come back. Some day. What kind of mother am I? Coping…. Rationalizing that their father will be home in two days, their grandmother will put in an appearance. Remember. Just until June.

I graduated with an Associate Degree in Nursing in June, passed the state boards, and began working as a Registered Nurse at Tillamook County General Hospital as a "float" nurse. I worked on the medical surgical ward, the obstetrical ward, and the intensive care unit.

July 6: I felt my mortality today. At the beginning of the night shift I assisted with the birth of a baby in the delivery room. Two people died a few hours later in ICU under my care. I felt their bodies, cold and heavy as I helped lift them onto the mortician's gurney. And it didn't bother me. Should it have?

My career as a Home Health/Hospice nurse began the following year and before long I was the Clinical Coordinator for the Home Health Department. I loved to visit my patients, some who were quite ill and dying in their homes. A family member usually met me at the door and would usher me into the home where I would provide care, comfort, and reassurance. "The nurse is here".

TWO PATIENTS: A CONTRAST

My job as a Home Health/Hospice nurse found me travelling Highway 101 along the Pacific Coast in Tillamook County. I saw patients in beach homes, in mountain shacks, farms, and cabins tucked away in the foothills of the coast range. Computer technology had not been developed for medical use and Nursing notes were all written by hand. I enjoyed relaxing at the edge of the Pacific Ocean and on the shore of Garibaldi Bay while writing my nursing notes.

Mary and Janet were both in their 40's and had been diagnosed with metastatic breast cancer. They had gastric tubes, foley catheters, Hickman "ports" in their chests (through which intravenous medications could be injected) and required daily dressing changes for abdominal incisions. They had undergone identical surgeries and shared the same oncologist. I was scheduled to see both women during the weekdays and I often visited on the weekends when it was my turn to be "on call".

Mary lived in Bay City with her husband and two teenage daughters. I sensed a spirit of peace upon entering their home. Mary lay in a hospital bed in the living room which was filled with flowers and soft classical music echoed throughout the home. She had travelled to Mexico where she had received an exotic naturopathic treatment for cancer, but the treatment had failed, and she was in the final stages of cancer. The family attended the local United Methodist Church and Mary spoke about how, after trying for so long to "beat" this cancer, she was at peace with herself and God. Mary accepted the difficult truth that she was dying, and she was done fighting. She was soft spoken and patient as I changed catheters, flushed intravenous lines, and changed dressings. The family was receptive as I gave guidance about how to provide for her physical and medical needs. I would find her well-cared for each time I visited and always left her home feeling uplifted.

Janet lived ten miles up Highway 101 in Rockaway with her husband. She was confined to a hospital bed in the living room where she could watch the ocean waves. She voiced a certainty that God was going to heal her, and she cited Bible scripture to justify this belief during my first visit. She would shout out demands to her anxious husband and he would hurry to bring her carrot juice (which she believed would cure her) and sips of water for which he never received any thanks.

Church members sat by her bed side or stood in the corner fervently praying for her healing. I was present a few times when the pastor came to sprinkle her with the "holy water of blessing", demanding loudly for the "forces of evil to leave". An air of desperation wafted through the home and I was always glad when I had completed my procedures and could leave. Janet began to decline rapidly and soon fell into a coma. Her husband tearfully turned to me and, as he realized the certainty of her impending death, said "she really is dying, isn't she?". She died a few hours later as he wept at her side surrounded by their fellow Christians.

Mary's life was ebbing away, but she still smiled weakly when I visited her for the last time in her home. She told me that she had lived a good life and knew she was going to Heaven. She was not afraid to die and felt confident that her husband would continue to care adequately for her daughters. As I helped her daughter roll Mary to her side, Mary cautioned me to "be careful. I don't want you to hurt yourself". She quietly died that evening while holding her husband's hand.

Two Christian families and two vastly different approaches to prayer, God, death, and dying. I had always been skeptical of those who prayed for the physical healing of others, especially when their prayers sounded more like demands than petitions. I had been part of such prayers a few times during my young adult years and had never been comfortable telling God what to do.

1985

October 8: Things change. So subtle. People change. I'm still in awe that I am a nurse. I'm enjoying the counseling portion of my work and, in fact, am thinking of obtaining a degree in counseling. I'm praying about this.

PART IV: THE JOURNALS

1986 - 1991

1986

DEPRESSION

January 15: How does change occur? When did I become who I am? Growth is so subtle that it may go undetected for an enormous length of time until one day the sun breaks through and, hello! I've changed! And so I curl up in a ball of guilt, chewing on a bag of chocolate chips, reading the comics, and watching TV while the ironing piles up and no one can find the scissors because they are in the junk drawer I've been meaning to clean for three months. I feel like an ant, standing at the bottom of Mt. St. Helens on May 17th and I know I have to make it to the top and back before it blows! I will continue to have this guilt, stronger at times and then less, and I will continue to be fat and unproductive and certainly not the creative joyful individual God intended for me to be!

April 7: As I stood looking out the window, I could clearly see four muddy fingerprints on the sill, reminding me to give Jonathan a housekey this morning so he won't have to crawl through the bedroom window again.

April 9: Feeling down down down. Like the Gnome from Nome was cold from the "inside out", I'm tired, sad from the inside-out. I feel like I'm under a dark cloud with no sunshine now and then to warm things up a bit. Right now, I don't want to work. Don't want to go anywhere....just want to stay home. But I can't. I can't. I can't. I've got to keep going. Keep going. Right now, the Lord must give me strength. I don't have it in myself, at least I don't think so. Okay now. Firm up. You are made in the Image of God. My self-worth is that of anyone. I'm no better or worse than another. Be yourself. (I'm trying). Strive to be all God wants you to be. Create. Feel. For others, feel. Begin to touch others in a special way. Allow God to work in and through you.

I had been in a three-month Mental Health rotation in nursing school at a psychiatric hospital where I had learned about mood disorders. I wondered if I would benefit from seeing a therapist and began seeing Dr. Larry Day, a Christian psychologist in Portland, who charged $120 for one hour of therapy. Cash. His theoretical premise was that we are all made in the image of God, and therefore we were created to create. He diagnosed me with Major Depressive Disorder, and I was relieved to know that I wasn't just crazy. I stopped seeing him after my third session.

April 16: I am not a weak person but a strong person with some weaknesses. I am not a bad person because of what I have or have not done, but a good person who made some bad choices. See the difference?

June 18: FAILURE. That is the one word that applies today. I have failed in my walk with you oh Lord. Again and again and again and again. I am no better spiritually than twenty years ago. Just playing the game better…smoother now. Acting the part, oh so false! O Lord, give me desire, give me burning, make me willing. Lord, forgive my laziness! Jesus touch me please. Heal me. Reveal in me Your Love.

We accompanied my parents to the Vancouver B.C. Expo in July. Thousands of people crowded the exhibits and we had to stand in line for hours to see the more popular exhibits. Beth and I were walking through the crowds one afternoon and I began to hear Calypso music. We turned the corner to see a Cajun band on a sequestered stage and we began to dance. The music was magical as we pranced and twirled and I felt free, so very free. I had not danced since high school and was surprised that music could be so energizing, so joy-giving. I thought "this is how I want to live, light, free, without the weight of life". I had tasted a new kind of joy and longed to experience it again. However, upon our return home, the familiar heaviness of angst continued to nip at my heels.

September 3:   *Down and Under*
                          Down and Out
                          Which way do I go?
                          Left or right?
                          Up or down?
                          This time I cannot know.
                          Purged of all wisdom
                          Stripped of all works

Now I lie naked before you.
With nothing. 33, almost 34. With nothing.
Save a smattering of modest achievement
Of small things done
Out of pride, zeal, greed, curiosity.
How much for You?
How much for others because I want to?
I am nothing.
I can do nothing alone.

November 13: A week of undisciplined living has passed, heaping guilt upon guilt. Oh Lord I feel I'm past forgiveness, so out of control, but I know that no one is ever past forgiveness! I know that.

Ron and I remained busy with a variety of commitments and interests in addition to our jobs. We were on the founding board of a shelter foster home for children, he was on the Tillamook Bay Community College Board of Directors, and I was on the Education Service District Parent Advisory Board. He started a few businesses and I was the Director of Music for the church and sat on the Spiritual Life Committee at the Netarts Friends Church.

1987

August 8: So deep down. I can hardly believe I'm actually this deep into despair. Specific self-destructive thoughts are so frightening and yet I cannot remember when my heart ached so and the tears stood so constantly ready to break loose. I feel so angry at everything and so helpless to affect change.

So here I sit looking for alternate ways out. I have no hope. No hope to ever change.

BAD DECISIONS

I was sitting with a hospice patient in her home when she asked if Ron and I would adopt her 14-year-old daughter after she died.

Martha had taken an EMT class from Ron and admired him for the kind and caring man that he was. I told Ron about her request and he insisted that we could not object to a dying request, that we were morally obligated to adopt her daughter. I was quite hesitant to disturb the flow of our life but wanted to be a good Christian.

Rebekka moved into our home during the final days of Martha's life and it was a disaster. She had been moved multiple times throughout her stormy life and, come to find out, was Martha's granddaughter, not her daughter. Rebekka was an angry child and, one day, her birth mother appeared out of nowhere to reclaim her.

A few months later one of the girls in the children's shelter home needed a foster home and Ron volunteered for us to take her. I was once again reluctant, especially after our experience with Rebekka. Debbie was older than our children, she terrorized Beth, and exposed Jonathan to unhealthy ideations and opinions. Her stay with us lasted only a few months. I had married Ron because of his kind heart and passion for justice, but I began to realize that we were not suited for all acts of kindness.

1988

September 20: Our marriage has never been on such shaky ground. It seems Ron and I just don't even think along the same lines, almost (not quite) like strangers. He's been stubborn, unrelenting in his views. Always so right it's infuriating. I even thought of leaving yesterday when I was so angry. Anger....there's been a lot around here. I hope we can overcome this.

BACK TO SCHOOL

Ron and I took turns attending college over a course of five years. He attended the first Paramedic school at Oregon Health Sciences University and became the first paramedic in Tillamook County. I had completed my Associate Degree in Nursing but wanted to obtain a Bachelor of Science Degree in Nursing (BSN). Nursing schools required that I complete an entire course of nursing, although I was already a Registered Nurse, and it would have taken me three more years (with constant travel to Portland) to complete a BSN.

1989

I decided to obtain a Bachelor of Arts Degree in Human Resource Management from George Fox College. Previous education and experience factored into degree completion, and I was able to attend one night-class a week with Saturday seminars once a month. Mom and Dad attended my graduation in May 1989 and, as I stood in my robe and cap while pictures were taken, Dad said, "what kind of degree can this be if it doesn't require a foreign language?"

May 28: My heart is heavy. It sags beneath the humid weight of fear and uncertainty.

Fatigued by a night of weeping, the wringing wretched kind that squeezes the soul to exhaustion.

Lord, I have asked forgiveness. And so it is not the heaviness of guilt that now stands squarely on my heart as it does when unconfessed sin fosters that guilt. No, I know you have forgiven. That is not in question.

PAIN – A SOLUTION

May 29: Side-ache = Vicodan. Did I need it? Probably not. I'm so afraid to throw them away knowing that isn't really the problem. I will get more. It is the motivation, the whys. Why do I think I need them? So fearful of no more.

Back injuries are notoriously common among nurses due to the physical demands of nursing. As a Home Health Nurse, I climbed on to a water-bed to insert a catheter, I bent over a patient lying on a mattress on the floor to draw a vial of blood, I climbed a ladder to a bunk bed to take a blood pressure and I assisted a 300# patient out of a tub. Once, when leaning down to take the blood pressure of an elderly gentleman seated in his low recliner, my back gave out and, suddenly I was sitting in his lap. Fortunately, he was nicely demented and laughed with glee as I struggled to stand. I was in the hospital for three days after that incident.

I had numerous bouts with back injuries and pain several times each year. In 1988 My doctor began prescribing a new pain medication in 1988 and by the spring of 1989 I was addicted to Vicodin. Unfortunately, the topic of substance abuse was not well-understood and famous celebrities had yet to step forward to describe their difficulties with alcoholism or drug addiction. I began to become concerned when I realized that I was reaching for a pill even when I didn't have any pain. I dishonestly told Doctor Betlinski that I still had pain when the pill bottle was almost empty, so that I could get more refills. I felt very guilty and began withdrawing from the world.

A guest preacher spoke at church one evening and described how the Devil systematically sabotages us with temptations specific to our weaknesses. He described an individual who had battled a propensity for alcohol abuse and how God had released him from this problem. I immediately recognized that this was what had been wrong all along: I was a bad Christian because I craved mind altering substances. The Devil was responsible for all my emotional and spiritual struggles! Since my marriage to Ron I had only consumed wine on a few rare occasions. I spoke with our pastor Jerry Baker after the service, sobbing that I was a sinner and that I needed help. Jerry came over to our house the next day to help me explain this to Ron. After speaking with my doctor, it was decided that I should attend a thirty-day residential substance abuse treatment program in Portland.

Looking back, I would not have needed to attend an in-patient substance abuse treatment program. Instead, I would have benefited from some education about addictive substances and my doctor could have worked with me to address pain management. However, this was 1989, and substance abuse facilities were gaining a foothold in the health care industry. The media was exposing the public to the topic of substance abuse and Betty Ford (President Ford's wife) had recently been interviewed about her problems with addiction. The medical industry was anxious to get on the recovery band wagon.

A NEW LIFE

Ron drove me to the New Day Substance Abuse Treatment Facility operated by the Seventh Day Adventist Medical system in Northeast Portland in the spring of 1989. The admission process included a search through my personal possessions (a suitcase and purse), a substance abuse assessment with one of the counselors and a cursory physical exam with the staff nurse. I was then told to join one of the discussion groups already in progress. The facilitator made introductions and I joined a circle comprised of ten males.

As they took turns speaking, I began to hear the "F" word. A lot. "F" this, "F'n" that. I was a sheltered church lady and had rarely heard that word spoken aloud. I was understandably quite shaken, and I stormed out of the room, marched to the front office and tearfully demanded to leave. I thought this was a Seventh Day Adventist (Christian) facility. How could they permit their patients to use such foul language? I was in the wrong place and didn't belong there. I was ushered back to the group with the assurance from the admissions director and the group facilitator that the other residents would be asked to refrain from using foul language. I did not hear the "F" word for the remainder of my stay.

I was surrounded by heroin and cocaine addicts and ex-felons. Many of them had lost marriages, homes, and livelihoods and had been arrested and/or hospitalized due to their substance abuse. The treatment facility staff questioned my reasons for being there and voiced the assumption that I must have, as a nurse, "diverted" (stolen) drugs on the job. It was humbling to introduce myself as an "addict and alcoholic" at the beginning of every group session but, as

I became familiar with my surroundings, I realized that we were all there for the same reason: we were vulnerable human beings who had experienced heartbreak and pain. I gained a great deal of perspective and tools for achieving emotional wellness during treatment and, for the first time, I no longer felt guilty. Most importantly, I learned to be honest with myself and others.

June 11: My first day at "New Day" treatment center! Leaving my family today was very difficult and I don't think I've ever been so nervous in my life. I'm also very afraid.

June 12: Many tears have been wept since yesterday which was horribly long with nothing to do but worry about whether I should be here. Today was just plain awful! So many young boys, everyone smokes, most use foul language.

June 15: How I lived through the first three days I'll never know. It was hell. My heart almost broke from the ache. I've never cried so much in my life.

I had never been away from my children for such a long time and I was relieved to be reunited with my family after the twenty-eight days of treatment. Our routine required a change upon my return home. The counselors had advised me to attend "90 A.A. meetings in 90 days" and I was determined to adhere to this advice.

July 17: This past week has been quite a harrowing experience. Quite simply, it was hell. I tried unsuccessfully to go to daily meetings while living a normally busy life. I almost died of fatigue and frustration.

July 29: I must remember to "keep it simple" when considering God. I have sensed God telling me that it is enough, for now, for me to accept that He is my Father and that I am His much-loved child. I must concentrate on that alone.

1990

Upon my return home, I began attending Alcoholic Anonymous meetings in Tillamook upon my return home and Dr. Parsons, a local internist, called and invited me to a recovery group for medical professionals. I started a Christian recovery group for the community at our church and took long walks on the beach. I had never been so happy, contented and fulfilled. I was at peace with myself and God.

In January, Beth and I joined the Tillamook Community Performing Arts community production of Fiddler on the Roof. She was one of the village girls and I was the Fiddler. I sat on a roof and danced on stage while playing my violin dressed as a little bearded Russian Jewish man. Ron was watching one of the performances and overheard an audience member comment, "he's a very good fiddler!" Ron turned around and informed them that "he" was a "she" and that he should know.

February 23, 1990: Playing "the Fiddler' has brought back a part of me I had lost. The thrill of performing, the flush of pride, the knowledge that not only can I do the job, but that I can do the job quite well. The comradery, the commitment as we draw near to the performance date…these have all restored some life to me.

Ron decided that, to assist my recovery and give me a new start, he would build a house in Netarts. He and his father finished the beautiful two-story home close to the beach by early spring. Mom and Dad came to see our new home and took a tour, up the stairs into the loft, down the stairs to the three bedrooms, into the living area with vaulted ceilings, and outside where our property was surrounded by a lush forest. Dad had little to say except, "there's no spigot for the back yard. How are you going to water your lawn?"

March 23: The house is so beautiful! I am in awe….overwhelmed that God would see fit to even let me live in such a place for a little while. I'm totally amazed, very humbled. Such a house I would've never expected to live in. Never.

March 8, 1990: Take a deep breath. Center down. Push the world away. Look Jesus in the face and think now about His love to me. Why am I here? What is my purpose? To be a fiddler? To dance a tune? To make the world smile? Lord, let me see me as you see me. Let me love me as You love me.

June 6, 1990: Everything is all right today. Today I am content. I like myself today and do not feel pressured. I have learned that I am worthy of God's love. I am not living under a cloud of guilt. I have learned to live today (am still learning). I am learning to keep my interpretations of events surrounding me simple. I pray the serenity prayer daily. Life somehow is brighter and clearer that it has ever been.

FATHER

Dad stopped by my office to take me out to lunch in September, and while I watched him drive away in his Toyota Corolla, wearing his golf cap, I was struck with the thought that I would never see him again. Our home was filled with teenagers who had just returned from a victorious Bible Quiz tournament on October 14th when my brother called me to tell me that my father had suffered an abdominal aortic aneurysm and was in critical condition at the Salem Hospital. I quickly packed a suitcase and, at the last minute, threw in my black dress.

Ron and I were sitting together in the ICU waiting room with Jane and Larry while Dad was in surgery. The surgeon appeared and told us that Dad had lost a lot of blood and that he probably wouldn't live through the next hour. We all sat in silence after the surgeon left the room and I closed my eyes. I heard Dad's voice saying, "Goodbye Phis (his nickname for me)". I voicelessly replied, "no Dad. You can't go, not yet. Please stay a little longer". The surgeon returned within minutes and said, "I don't know why, but the bleeding has stopped, and he has stabilized. If you want to see him, I suggest you visit right now".

Ron and I rose without hesitation and were led into an ICU room full of noisy machines. I didn't recognize my father at first due to swelling and edema but then I saw the turquoise ring on his right ring finger. His eyes were closed as I took his hand. I assured him that I would stay by his side. When I asked if he could hear me, he squeezed my hand. After a while, Larry and Jane came into the room and stood at the foot of the bed. Larry spoke with a flat tone and thanked him for "teaching me how to be a man, for teaching me how to work hard". Then he and Jane left the room. Ron took his hand and said "Claude, I want you to know that I will always be here for Jessymae. You don't have to worry about her. I'll take care of her".

I remained with Dad all night and into the next day, and I whispered to him to "follow the light" as the beeps from the cardiac monitor indicated that his heart was failing. Ron stepped out of the room for a few minutes and I sang Amazing Grace to him as he died. I removed his ring and Ron and I helped the nurse prepare his body for transport to the Stayton funeral home.

October 26: My father suffered a ruptured aortic (abdominal) aneurysm from which he died on October 15th. The ensuing days have been filled with the business of burying and the eventual day-to-day grappling with heart-pain . I am profoundly stricken with an emptiness, a hollow sensation that echoes images of a father distantly and recently known. Memories from the far past transport me to a five-year-old state of emotional lability. Sitting on my father's lap ("Daddy") and then riding in the car, talking with a confident new-to-college voice, smelling his pipe and thinking I may vomit from the smell as we hit the curvy road but too nice, too polite, to really say anything. And then late at night a know-it-all sixteen-year-old questioning the values of middle America. Sitting up very late, speaking intently in front of the dying fire as we argued, no, debated our points of view concerning all those things so important to him like patriotism, the work ethic, responsible world citizenship. And I, knowing I was attempting to compete with the expert, sought to define why warring on foreign soil to defend another country may be wrong, why I could not condone ever taking up arms to defend even my home. Why making money and acquiring a potentially lucrative degree was immaterial to a person's worth. And somewhere, on some plane, we did eventually agree. I am aware today of how much we agreed on the very important things of life. He was my reasoning mentor, he taught me to process, to think through, to be fair.

Mother was never the same after my father's death. She was not prepared to live life without the man she loved and was bewildered that God would allow him to die. She became increasingly withdrawn and depressed and I soon realized that I had lost both parents when my father died.

Our new home was constantly abuzz with pubescent and teenage children, meetings, and parties. Evenings were spent by the fire reading and visiting with one another. Ron continued to work as a paramedic and was teaching EMT classes while I was busy with work, various community interests and church responsibilities.

December 31: Mother came and stayed five very long days. Emotional, stressful, but necessary for healing to take place. I suppose the worst thing is how much I hurt for mom. I suffer when she suffers, and I can't fix it.

1991

January 25: War broke out on January 16th. US didn't take any extra time. I have marched in a peace rally, attended a peace supper…I'm more committed to a peace testimony than I have ever been. The media coverage suggests that I am in the minority. I can't believe it. However, my stand is based on religious conviction, not political. We must not kill. Absolutely. I can see no argument to convince me that my life is of more value than another, that I have the right, as a human, to declare life or death for another fellow human, no matter how evil his or her actions may be.

August 4: Today. One day. The only day I have. The rattling of inner despair has subsided. Peace/serenity are filling its place. Learning to live today, relearning not to obsess into tomorrow or backwards to yesterday. That is the only way to find peace.

The day is calm. The sound of the ocean mumbles in the distance, just as the regrets of yesterday and the unknowns of tomorrow echo through time. But I will not heed them. Not today. For today God is my strength, my fortress. He alone will save me and I rest in his soft fluffy wings. Today.

August 14: I am intrigued with the thought of returning to George Fox for an advanced degree in psychology. Dear Lord, not my will but Yours! Help me to keep things in perspective. Today is all I have.

Later that month our family went on a camping trip to Lost Lake in Central Oregon with Ron's family.

BOOK 2

PART I: THE JOURNALS

1991 - 1995

THE WRECK

November 13: And today I will watch a little blond-haired girl be buried. Falls are becoming not such a good time of year. On November 8th I struck a small child with my car and she died the next day. Unavoidable, unbelievable, unthinkable. "That which I feared the most has come upon me" (Job). God has given me strength for each day. Oh Lord walk with me today. Stay close- let me feel the sweetness of your holy breath as I walk through this next event (which I can't avoid). Lord, prepare the way for me. Go before me and behind me. Lift me up, give me good and perfect utterance. Let me say the right things to the mother, the father. I will never be the same.

Eight days after the wreck I was sitting in the car waiting for Ron while he shopped for groceries at Thriftway. My spiral notebook from work was in the backseat and I was overcome with an overwhelming urge to write the following:

November 16: I woke up on November 8th dripping with sweat, trying to shake away an awful nightmare: I was a passenger in a vehicle driven by a young lady who unknowingly ran over a little girl. I screamed for her to stop and jumped out of the car to find a blond-haired girl lying peacefully in the road. The dream dogged me, and I shuddered as I considered how very awful that would be, how I could never emotionally survive the impact of knowing a life was lost and that I was an instrument of that loss.

I packed my Geo Metro with the nursing supplies necessary to administer chemotherapy to Mrs. Wallace who lived on the East side of town. It was 3:30 P.M. and the medication was due to be administered at 4:00. I turned left out of the hospital parking lot on to 3rd street and noticed a little boy and girl tussling on the sidewalk.

I thought I was in a dream again.

A surprised little face appears at the right of my fender, then, like a rag doll, the little girl hits the hood of my car, and slides off. I am aware that my car has stopped and is sitting sideways facing a house. I rapidly turn off the ignition, unstrap my seatbelt, and step out of the car, hoping that I will not find what I fear I will find. *Slap Slap Slap.* My shoes echo sharply in the silence. There she is, the blond little girl in my dream, lying on her left side, very peacefully, naturally. "Honey can you hear me?! Wake up!" Then she emits an expiratory grunt and I see blood coming from her mouth. "Wake up!" I feel for a carotid pulse. Yes. Strong and throbbing. I can't turn her head - she might have a neck fracture. My medical training automatically takes over. I had been on my way to care for a cancer patient, to prolong her life and now this life before me is ebbing away. Must use the tilt chin method I tell myself instinctively. One, two...please breathe! I look up to see a small boy, standing on the sidewalk, staring. Probably her brother. "Hurry! Call 911!" I scream. He runs off as I resume respirations. Still strong carotid. The face mask in my nursing bag is of little use now since it would take precious moments to retrieve it from the car.

A large blond-haired woman runs towards the child. "My baby!" She pushes me away to lean over the little girl. "I'm a nurse" I say. "Please let me help her!" Then the mother disappears. I can sense activity, cars, sirens. Breathe. Breathe. Good pulse. A large presence appears at my right. It's Jack, an off-duty paramedic. "Here Jack, you take over, you can do this better than me." He hesitates. There's blood all over and I don't have a face mask. The ambulance screeches to a stop and two paramedics jump out. Jack is doing respirations now. "She's got a strong carotid" I cry. "A strong carotid!". And it is now that I begin to acknowledge what has happened.

A small figure steps from the crowd of bystanders. I don't know this woman, but I collapse into her arms. I feel safe holding on to her. Don't let me go. A policeman rushes over. "Has anyone called her husband? Who is her husband?" I look up and say, "You know me Tom!" "Oh, it's you Phyllis!". I had lived in Tillamook for fourteen years and moved in many circles. I felt safe even in this crowd of onlookers. "It's Phyllis Hays". The fire chief's wife had been watching me administer aid to the child and told me later than she had said to herself, "Good, Phyllis is here. She'll know what to do". She didn't know I had been the driver.

"I dreamed this would happen" I cry as a few bystanders help me to the house. "I *really did. I dreamed it! Why God?!" I collapse on a couch and notice the blood splattered on my glasses and down the front of my blouse. Am I bleeding? No this is her blood, still wet. I notice a large bump on my forehead.*

My pastor arrives, then my husband, the paramedic and I ask, "is she going to live Ron?" "No, probably not." My 17-year old son appears, pausing at the door. When he was learning to drive, I had cautioned him to be careful, especially when children were anywhere around. I emphasized that striking a child (or anyone for that matter) would be the worst thing that could ever happen. Unthinkable. So now I say, "the most awful thing in the whole wide world has happened!" "I know" he whispers as he wraps his arms around me and leads me to the car.

Jonathan drove me home from the scene of the wreck and we arrived to find Linda Kelly, my friend from church, making a pot of coffee in our kitchen. Dr. Ann, my doctor, called to ask how I was feeling. I told her I had a bump on my forehead, and she instructed me to return to the hospital to be assessed for a head injury. She met me at the hospital and as she examined my pupils, she told me that Kristine had been taken by ambulance to a Portland Hospital. I wasn't surprised the following morning when Dr. Ann called again, this time to tell me that Kristine had died. Her family had kept the machines keeping her alive long enough to ensure that Kristine's heart, liver, and kidneys could be harvested for donation.

Many visitors dropped by during the following week to give me their condolences and love. Hot dishes and desserts were left at our home, just as if I had lost a loved one of my own. Pastor Jerry Baker abandoned his sermon plans on Sunday, November 10th so that the church could spend the hour of worship in prayer for me and Kristine's family. He told me later that a gentleman visiting our church for the first time "gave his life to Christ" because of the congregation's testimony of love and compassion. Good for him.

The adult brother of Kristine, the little girl, called to say that their family understood that it was just an accident and that he would be praying for me. My brother Larry called (probably because he felt obligated to) and told me that I should be prepared to be sued. The hospital administrator called to ask if I needed anything and I told him I thought I should stay home from work for a while. I received over one hundred cards and many flowers from concerned townspeople. Amnesia erases critical moments of the accident, but brake marks indicated appropriate speed. The county DA wrote "The accident was unavoidable".

One afternoon the police chief visited our home about one week after the accident. He was concerned because Kristine's family was "known" to the legal community. She had several siblings, all with different fathers, and they were a "rough bunch". He warned us to be careful, and to look out for our children. Jonathan came home from high school a few days later and told Ron that he had been harassed by two of Kristine's older brothers. He said that he was "all right, it's no big deal". But I was worried.

November 27: Things are hard. Life is not so easy. God is still with me and I will not forsake Him. He loves me and I seek to return His love. I am recovering from a trauma just as anyone recovers from a physical trauma. I will be in a time of healing then will emerge renewed, built up, and stronger for the experience.

December 8: It's taken me ten takes to put a new message on our answering machine, one with Silent Night with a cheerful greeting, but it is a struggle to sound cheerful, so I recorded the message over and over again until my voice sounded happy enough. My heart is always heavy and sometimes I struggle to breathe, but now I've gone back to work, one foot ahead of the other.

I came home from work a few days later and checked the answering machine for messages. "How can you be so cheerful after what you did to my little girl? You murdered her! Go to hell!" We changed our phone number.

December 12: Will I be stronger? Over a month later and the pain sears deeply.

At times it feels like my breath is being squeezed from me. I continue, though, one foot following the other, plodding along through life's daily events and chores. Christmas is coming and it's unavoidably near. I'm going through the motions but would rather postpone it for a while. I'd like to crawl into a warm friendly cave for a few weeks to wait all "this" out ......just let it pass (like hibernation) and when I emerge the sun will shine warmly on me, my heart will be lifted, and the pain will be forever gone. Healing is not like that. It must begin deep within and progress outward.

December 23: Why is it so hard to write? So much has happened – events, images swirl around my mind, lashing at my thoughts, tumbling my emotions along – first low, then lower, then upside-down, but never high. Who am I in this? Where do I fit? What can I do? Why me? They think I'm "fine" now. (Because that's what feels best). Keep forging ahead, faithful – One step at a time. Reaching for (and finding) the hand holds when I slip. Search for the hope and find it in Christ, who suffered as I do now. Someone understands.

THEOLOGICAL JOLT

Jonathan was a senior at Tillamook High School and was on the varsity basketball team. We were attending one of his games when a gentleman approached. I recognized him from community church gatherings as one of the leaders in the local Nazarene Church. He hugged me warmly and said, "I'm so glad God allowed this to happen to you! Now, as a Christian, you can be a testimony to everyone about the faithfulness of God". I was appalled. Was God responsible for this?

1992

January 12: It is so hard to journal. Pain sears many common acts and I often feel breathless, struggling to breathe past the large tear in my throat.

January 19: What is the wisdom of today? Suffering – pain, heart-ache....must be an individual solitary experience. Alone it pierces deep and the hole gapes beneath me threatening to eat me whole. Calling to God, pleading for strength must be an individual solitary experience.

April 15: The cement of despair is quickly hardening around my heart. I'm not sure I want out. Just cover me up and we'll be finished playing this game. How can I hide from death, from the loneliness of loss and hopelessness? I'm tired of death, of bad, uncomfortable things. I'm tired of aches, of gray hair. I'm tired of purposeless movements, the going to work to make money so I can live in a home so I can sleep so I can go to work. Where's purpose? Where's meaning? Solomon was right: "There's no new thing under the sun". Where are you God? I know you're here, but my eyes are clouded with doubt, fear, lack of faith. Dear Lord, please restore me to sanity and renew my spirit within me.

WE HAVE TO MOVE

I was standing at the stove stirring pasta noodles when a police officer came to our home. Ron answered the door and, after speaking with him for a moment, said "Phyllis, come here." I stood, frozen in place. I knew why he was here. "You just take the papers", I said. "No, you have to take them".

May 1: I'm being sued. That does not feel good at all. Ron had warned me this would probably happen and so did Larry. An officer knocked on our door, established my identity, and handed me an official document describing in legalese why and for how much I was being sued. "Being served papers". I had heard the phrase and until now did not appreciate the emotional impact of that simple phrase. Although the accident occurred almost six months ago, I knew I would probably be sued at some time simply because I happened to be at the wrong place (on a busy street) at the wrong time (when a child decided to dash out in front of my car). A tragic accident that could not be avoided. Yet, the parents, in their anger, loss, and frustration are still looking for answers. Why? How? And maybe by filing a suit they hope to find their answers.

I was sitting in the hospital cafeteria when Cheryl, the community mental health center social worker, sat down at my table. "I have to talk to you". She facilitated a grief support group and was "legally required" (Tarasoff Rule) to share that Kristine's mother had threatened to injure or kill my daughter Beth.

August 26: Decisions have been made to move. Things are hurling fast....we are moving before the house sells, an illogical move. But we must.

We borrowed my father-in-law's small travel trailer and parked it up on a foggy mountain above Gaston, behind the home of the Muhrs, a family we had met at the Quaker Family Camp. Jonathan left for his freshman year at George Fox College and Beth began attending Yamhill-Carlton High School. We had no phone, no television, and took our showers in the Muhr's home. I quickly found a job as a Home Health Nurse at Newberg Hospital and Ron began working at a home for mentally disturbed children.

September 13: Feeling desperate again. Wanting to change circumstances. Afraid, wondering. How are things going to work out? Where will we live? Who will be in our lives? How are you going to do this God? How much more can I stretch!

November 17: The past few months have been difficult (to say the least!). But we are (I am) managing. We have been perched up here on Olson Road in Gaston since August 29th. We are in the process of purchasing a house right in the heart of Yamhill, across from the high school. I'm on antidepressants and am seeing a psychologist almost weekly. I think I'm doing much better! I even started exercising! I've turned 40 since last writing.

November 18: Dear God, you know the ins and outs of my life. You smile at my joys and cry when I am sad. You know how it feels because you've been there. You know ten-fold what I'm going through.

We moved into a two-story Tudor style house on the main street of Yamhill just before Christmas. It was a musty old home in disrepair, but, with new floors, paint, a new oil furnace and lacy curtains it soon became our home.

1993

TRANSITION

February 26: I'm excited about the future! For the first time in 1 ½ years I have a plan, a dream. It is a very big dream! But I'm making plans to proceed. I will not be content to stay where I am professionally. I must move on.

I had finally decided to become a psychologist. I applied to the George Fox College Graduate School of Psychology, began taking psychology classes and studied for the Graduate Record Examination (GRE). We joined West Chehalem Friends Church where I played the piano for worship service and served on the Elders (Spiritual Life) Committee, and I was working full time as a Home Health Nurse. Life was full but dark clouds loomed.

March 25: The day started with an earthquake! (5.4 on the Richter Scale). I really didn't have time to be frightened until afterwards when I realized my kids were at Netarts. It was more awe-inspiring than anything....the ultimate in powerlessness! I called later and the kids are fine.

June 2: My attorney left a message for me at work. Since the pre-trial hearing was to be in June, I assumed that was what it was about and was fearful of calling. I was so chicken I had Ron call Friday morning. Ron called at work to tell me "It's over. They settled in court!" Praise God!

August 19: We're here at the Inn of the 7th Mountain in Bend. Jon brought Tiffany (his girlfriend) and Beth brought Shannon, her friend and Tiffany's sister. All day raft trip yesterday. Expensive but exhilarating. What a great experience! I found a pushed-out screen and window propped up with a book in the girl's room this morning. Of course, I was at first alarmed (who had broken in?) but realized that the girls had planned an escapade during the night. Had they gone out on a secret liaison? I checked the girls: All accounted for. What has happened to my sweet innocent little girl? Has she changed to a devious conniving rebellious creature?

Beth and her friend Lisa were on the Yamhill High School soccer team and were at practice one wet stormy day after school. I drove up to the field so Beth wouldn't have to walk home in the cold rain. She and Lisa were rolling down the muddy hill together, having a great messy time.

November 12: I had a weird thing happen to me yesterday. I was waiting for Lisa and Beth as they were rolling down the hill all covered with mud, and I had the thought "Lisa had better be careful or she'll lose the baby".

Beth told me two weeks later than Lisa had just found out that she was pregnant with her boyfriend's baby. Just like my mom, I had a psychic sense. I continue to experience this psychic "knowing" on occasion. I don't look at specific women and wonder if they're pregnant but, rather, I'll be introduced to a woman or just glance at someone I barely know. Somehow, I know. I've never been wrong.

November 15: What a precious child Beth is! I love her so much. I pray every day for her, that she will become the child of God she was created to be…that she will always seek a holy life and never lose her basic personality, her capacity to love others.

1994

February 3: A lot of "wreck" memories today. I just need daily meditation and prayer to spiritually survive.

March 29: I got the letter and I've been accepted (to graduate school)! Now my life takes some interesting twists as I prepare.

May 23: I've been in a deep hole. I get so down, my face seems unable to turn toward any light, preferring to peer into darkness and despair.

July 24: "You'll only know heavenly deliverance after you've experienced divine discomfort". Hebrews 12:12.

August 4: Ron is gone for a month to Zaire to care for the suffering refugees from Rwanda. I've never feared for Ron's life before like now. It's a very unsafe situation, extremely dangerous.

THEOLOGICAL CONFLICTS

August 31: First day of (graduate) school. I wish Ron was here to share it with me.

Ron returned safely from his life-changing medical mission, and I felt a renewed love for my amazing husband. I resigned from my nursing job, started school, 1 and threw myself into academic pursuits. Jonathan continued to excel at George Fox, majoring in computer science. Beth was busy as a high school junior participating in Mock Trial, Jazz choir, and softball. Our home was frequented by her friends from high school. When we held a surprise 16th birthday party for Beth over thirty teenagers were in attendance.

George Fox College was a Christian college and I began to take the mandatory theology and Bible courses required for my degree. I began to learn how to scholarly pursue Biblical writings and was stunned to realize that everything I had learned about the Scriptures was not necessarily true. I had been taught that literally every single word of the Bible was true, I had memorized the names of all of the books of the Bible when I was a child, and I could recite hundreds of Kings James Version scripture verses. I had read the entire Bible through at least twelve times and my Bibles were dog-eared and worn. To question the contents of the Bible meant certain damnation.

I learned from Howard Macy, one of my favorite Bible professors, that "Bibleidolotry" is the term used to describe the act of revering the Bible as a holy object. I had recited the "Pledge of Allegiance to the Bible" in Sunday School, and my mother wouldn't allow any object (i.e. a piece of paper) to be placed atop a Bible because "that would be sacrilege". We treated the Bible as if it held some sort of magical power and the implication was that "desecration" of this object would bring certain damnation to anyone who dared to mistreat it.

A large picture of bearded monks sitting at a table writing on scrolls with an angel hovering above had hung on the walls of our Sunday School room. So, I had assumed that God had spoken audibly to this group of men as they wrote down every sacred word. But I began to learn from Bible scholars and theologians that the Bible was a human creation based on lore passed down through the ages on ancient scrolls and parchments found in dusty chambers and caves. I was surprised to learn (and embarrassed that I hadn't wondered about any of this) that all religions are human constructs designed to better understand the Universe and all of life, and I was forced to reconsider the biblical underpinnings of my theological convictions.

1995

April 4: The more I learn the less I know so I must seek the truth! Continue searching for the LIGHT. God will give me direction if I am willing.

July 13: I am theologically baffled – questioning all I have been taught. Jesus Christ – Who is He? God – Who is He/She? The Bible – Is it the only Holy Book and how errant is it? To Who and What must I hold to be true? Real truth….. I am praying.

RE-AWAKENED MEMORIES

One day in June during summer break, I was heading to Newberg from home and came around a sharp corner to see four dead geese in the road. Two other geese wandered aimlessly through the carnage and occasionally poked at the dead geese as if trying to wake them up. Everyone in town knew that this was the "goose corner" and that one needed to slow down for the family of geese that crossed the road throughout the day. But someone had plowed into the entire flock. I was dizzy and suddenly, instead of geese, I saw little blonde girls sprawled on the road. I sat in my car, frozen, as other drivers stopped and removed the dead birds. Traffic resumed and cars honked as they passed while I sat there in a daze. My heart felt heavy and I couldn't breathe. I finally turned the car around and headed back home. That night my dreams were full of death and darkness.

Anxiety gripped me, nightmares tore into my sleep, and intrusive thoughts badgered me during the day. I was filling my car with gas one day when my chest began to ache, and I was unable to breathe. I thought I was having a heart attack. A gas station attendant called an ambulance, and after one night in the hospital, I was advised that my heart was fine. I had had a panic attack.

Ron and Beth had been accepted to join the Northwest Medical Team on a trip to a Romanian orphanage and would be gone for a whole month. I couldn't tolerate the emotional pain any longer and, within an hour of kissing them goodbye at the airport I had purchased two bottles of wine. My plan was to numb myself for just a while, just during their absence. I needed a reprieve from the pain.

INTERVENTION

August 13: Drink. It brings me a degree of temporary relief. And I don't feel at all remorseful. I must gain control, but heartache – sometimes so deep – It is a relief to hide from it.

August 27: In the mornings I am resolute. No more. And I hear the voices of my loved ones in Romania. And I know that, if nothing else, I cannot let them down. But then the pain begins. Again. The memories.

August 29: Two times hugging the toilet yesterday. Not pretty, quite unpleasant.

I was sitting in my recliner in the living room passed out with a textbook in my lap. A glass lay on its side, and red wine dripped from the pages and onto the floor when Jonathan and Tiffany walked into the living room. I was startled and then appalled when my son gently awakened me. He had come to check on me because we had spoken on the phone earlier that day and he was alarmed with the slurring of my speech. So, there they were. He phoned a friend of our family, Keith Lamm, who was good friends with the director of a nearby substance abuse treatment facility. Within hours I was seated in the intake room at Springbrook Treatment Center talking with a substance abuse counselor. The Oregon State Board of Nursing required a 90-day treatment protocol for nurses requiring a second round of treatment. I didn't return home until the middle of January.

Springbrook Treatment Center in Newberg was a "specialty" treatment center for professionals and anyone else who could afford to be there. Doctors, dentists, pharmacists, and nurses made up the roster of patients in addition to attorneys, celebrities, their offspring, and individuals connected to the entertainment industry.

One day a man wearing a fedora and a flowing cape arrived in a black limousine. He grasped the large brass eagle at the top of his cane and sauntered through the front door of the facility past the Intake Office and towards the resident lounge. I had observed his grand entrance with some other residents and Judy, a fellow nurse and resident, told him he didn't belong in the lounge and that he needed to return to the front office. "Don't you know who I am!?", he said. "Yes" she replied. "You're a fuckin' addict!" It turns out that he was some big movie director from Hollywood. He abruptly left when cocaine was found inside the brass eagle on his cane.

A NEW ADDICTION

One evening I was relaxing on the back porch (where most of the residents had retreated to smoke) when I asked to "borrow" a cigarette from Pam, a pretty little blonde with permanent eyeliner. She said, "I thought you didn't smoke" as she handed me a Virginia Slims Menthol cigarette. "It doesn't matter anymore," I replied as I lit it up. She warned me "Menthols are the worse. You'll never quit once you start". She was right.

Ron, upon learning of my admission to substance abuse treatment, decided that he and Beth should disrupt their mission, and they returned home a few days later. I was talking to him on the facility pay phone and casually mentioned that I had smoked a cigarette. He absolutely lost it! He spoke words I had never heard from him lips. This Quaker man who forbade our children to say "Darn" and "Gosh" was using the "F" word. He was livid, and obviously more concerned about my smoking than he was about my "need" for substance abuse treatment. This was not the Ron I knew.

I'M SCREWED

Here I was in Substance Abuse Treatment. Again. School was scheduled to resume in a few weeks, and I was screwed. I was suffering from constant anxiety: Thoughts from the wreck tore through every waking hour and nightmares and terrors haunted my sleep. I was administered the MMPI II (The Minnesota Multiphasic Personality Inventory - second revision) by the staff psychologist who diagnosed me with acute Posttraumatic Stress Disorder. I was not, however, offered the opportunity to receive psychotherapy while at Springbrook. Instead, I was required to attend group sessions which always began with the requisite introduction: "I'm Phyllis and I'm an alcoholic".

During my third week of treatment, Ron surprised me with a visit in the middle of the week. He asked if I had seen the newspaper that day and I told him, "no". He tearfully told me that his cousin Laura and her children had been murdered in Scotts Mills by Laura's estranged husband the previous day. Laura had called Ron in July to ask for some advice because her husband had become increasingly domineering and physically abusive. She feared for her safety, and Ron had invited her to come live with us for a while, but she had declined the offer. Instead, she moved in with her mother in Scotts Mills. Her husband, David, had engaged in ongoing "counseling" from his pastor who insisted that David had a biblical obligation to be the "head" of the household. David had received a restraining order to stay away from Laura and the children on the day before the shootings and he was convinced that no matter what the cost, he should be reunited with his family.

David fired fatal shots into Laura, 35 years old, Sarah, 6 years old, and Rachel 3 years old, after he broke into the home. He then stepped outside and shot the six-month old daughter dead as Laura's mother Margaret tried to run away with baby in April her arms. As David aimed the gun towards himself, a neighbor jumped over the hedge and tackled him to the ground. I attended the sentencing hearing several months later where David ranted about how he had killed his family with the intention of joining them in Heaven. But his plans for suicide had been thwarted by the neighbor. David did us all a favor and hung himself in jail the following Spring.

I have often wondered how much this event contributed to Ron's crumbling ability to cope during that very difficult time in our lives.

October 15: Today is the 5th anniversary of my father's death. I really miss him. Things have been so strange since he died. Life has been so hard, so many things have happened, so many very bad things! It seems that his death ushered in all these horrid events. I accept, surrender to the program today, now. There is no reason to fight and kick. I am powerless. Totally. I accept, surrender to the prescribed treatment program of Springbrook. I do not have to understand why or even agree with the rationale. I am being broken by authority. If that is God's will, I accept that.

October 17: I feel like I'm on the edge. Just about to topple. Defenseless. All of my strength has been stripped away. Now I'm empty. A big zero. Nothing is left but vapor. I'm afraid, so afraid.

October 23:   I went on a walk searching for a reason to live.
I found a solitude that engulfed me, circling, surrounding
Then driving the trauma of yesterday, the dread of tomorrow
Into my brain, my frontal lobes
and beyond until the heaviness of hopelessness numbed my soul.

I went on a walk searching for a reason to live
And found nothing left of my life....
No reason to live.

November 8: I talked to God today. I waited for an answer, a comforting touch, a moment of clarity. I was very disappointed and feel I cannot go on. The pain is so heavy. I feel like I'm going to suffocate. The heaviness is inescapable. God help me. Psalms 51:10-12: Create in me a clean heart O God and renew a right spirit within me. Cast me not away from thy presence O Lord and take not your Holy Spirit from me. Restore unto me the Joy of your salvation and renew a right spirit within me.

I had been separated from my family for several months except for sporadic visits on weekends with family and I cherished my time with Beth and Jon; but I began to dread seeing Ron. He was angry with me and continued to berate me for smoking. He didn't seem to comprehend that I was suffering and didn't understand that I continued to experience emotional trauma related to the wreck.

1996

January 11: I'm afraid to go home. I'm afraid not to go home. I don't know if I love Ron. I don't think so. But I care deeply for him and have the highest respect for him. I am angry I have to feel these feelings, very angry. I'm afraid of success, of making it. Easier to fail and get it over with.

HOME AGAIN BUT....

January 16: I'm home. Trying to be honest, to be true to myself. Truth: I don't know if I love Ron and these past two days have been super tense. Truth: I like smoking and don't want to stop. Truth: I'd rather live alone. I don't feel that I'm giving as much to Ron as he is to me. Now he is being super patient and kind. But I feel "less than", like I don't deserve all this. I feel like a selfish brat.

February 6: We are buying Gramma Magee's house in Scotts Mills. Just smoked three cigarettes yesterday. Today should be less.

February 18: I feel like Ron isn't even trying and that I must do all the changing. In fact, I think the main reason I'm trying to quit smoking is to escape his "judgment'. I feel like crap when he tosses inuendoes at me. He has no concept, no empathy for addictions and the process of ceasing an addictive behavior. I think underneath it all he's saying, "just quit". I sense disdain and pity, not encouragement and unqualified love.

Beth was half-way through her senior year of high school when I returned home. Her father had become emotionally distant during my absence and she was left alone at home while he was away for days at a time for his paramedic job. She sometimes stayed with friends but generally fended for herself. I felt responsible for abandoning her and was eager to restore security and emotional support to her life.

February 22: Beth is home sick. Time with Beth has been very good. I've been able to devote one-on-one listening -fixing food she likes, rubbing her head, listening. It's nice to be able to mother without multiple distractions and pressures.

February 27: Dear Ron, I'm sitting here feeling bruised and battered. Your unpredictable anger frightens me. Just when I think things are okay you become unreasonably angry. It's very hard to let down with you, to trust you, when I am periodically the recipient of your tantrums. I feel like you feel the need to retaliate and punish me.

TATTOO TIME

One warm March day, I drove to Salem to visit Jean, a heavily tattooed attorney and one of my fellow residents from Springbrook. We decided to take a ride with the top down in her convertible. We passed a tattoo parlor as we motored west on Highway 22 and I commented, "I've always wanted a tattoo on my ankle, a tattoo of a leaf of ivy". The brakes screeched as she did a U-turn and headed back toward the tattoo parlor. I didn't know that this establishment was where she had received most of her tattoos. "This lady wants a tattoo and she wants it now," she said to the gentleman at the counter. I had a green tattoo of an ivy leaf on my right ankle within 30 minutes. I would get four more tattoos over the next twenty years.

The marital relationship was becoming increasingly strained and Ron was irritable much of the time. He was frustrated that I wouldn't quit smoking. I, however, found smoking to be a convenient tool for maintaining emotional and physical distance from him.

March 4: It's difficult to love someone you fear. Ron is due home any moment and I dread his return, yet I anticipate it, hoping he will be jovial and positive yet fearing he will be negative and judgmental.

I had filed a Workman's Compensation Claim in order to pay for the hefty cost of my three-month residency at Springbrook. I obtained a copy of my treatment records in order to make the case that PTSD symptoms (related to the wreck which had occurred while working) had contributed to the circumstances leading up to my admission to treatment. Jean helped me obtain legal counsel to assist with my claim and, in order to proceed with the claim, I had obtained the records from my stay at Springbrook.

March 18: I read all of Springbrook's progress notes about me today. I was labelled "grandiose" as well as "possible Personality Disorder", although no one ever evaluated me for it. In addition, they seem to think that I was drinking when I had the wreck. Mary Francis, the nun ("spiritual counselor"), wrote that I had a "black-out" right before the wreck.

April 20: I am resentful towards the Springbrook staff for not addressing my PTSD and accusing me of using before the wreck. They skewed my treatment plans and displayed disdain towards me in their writings. I am angry at them for wasting time and causing me trauma. I am angry at everyone for not believing me.

Staff at substance abuse treatment centers during the 1990's were only required to have some sort of Associate or Bachelor degree and, more importantly, needed to be in recovery from alcoholism and/or drug addiction. Most of them had been schooled in the rooms of Alcoholics Anonymous and applied the black and white principles of the "twelve steps" to their clinical approach. These individuals had little professional education in the domain of psychology. They ethically had no right to render a mental health diagnosis.

Personality Disorders should only be diagnosed with psychometric evaluations and extended periods of behavioral observations and assessments by trained mental health professionals (psychologists and psychiatrists). Personality <u>traits</u> differentiate humans from one another and there are no "good" or "bad", or "normal" traits. A <u>personality disorder</u>, on the other hand, is a long-standing pattern of unhealthy and dysfunctional behavior that has caused relational and/or legal difficulties for the individual and those around him/her. Personality traits tend to become situationally exaggerated and may mimic a personality disorder during times of stress and/or illness. I have no doubt that I presented as very needy and histrionic during those initial days at Springbrook and understand why an untrained staff member may have wondered whether I was "personality disordered". But they had no right to document such speculations in my medical record.

Beth rallied during the second half of her senior year. Our home had settled back into a comfortable rhythm and I was able to provide a nice balance of guidance and nurturing since I wasn't working or attending school.

May 30: Beth's last day of school! Unbelievable! Just yesterday we walked her to school for her first day of 1ˢᵗ grade and rejoiced together that she was beginning her school experience. I'm feeling sad…..so many changes! My children are leaving me….

June 2: Beth sang so beautifully at graduation. I am so proud of her!

SCOTTS MILLS FARM

Ron's grandmother had died during the previous year and her sons offered Ron, the oldest male grandson, the opportunity to buy the property for $30,000. We began to prepare for our move to Grandma Magee's house in Scotts Mills, an old farmhouse situated on six acres up on a hill overlooking green fields and pastures with an old neglected orchard. It was a tranquil haven set apart from the rest of the world. I found solace there, especially when Ron was gone.

June 9: Up at the farm (in Scotts Mills). Alone. God, let me not be swept away by events and circumstances, rather help me to flow with whatever comes into my life today. I feel God closer than I have for a long time. Spiritual breath is beginning, once again, to flow in me. I don't need to understand my theology, but I do need to strive to draw close to God, who as, usual, waits patiently.

June 30: We moved yesterday. We had a great crew: Noel, Amy, Tim, John Hays (father-in-law), Jonathan...Really great to have so much help! Beautiful sunny day. Must re-center, focus. Stressful time now. Too tired for too long. I'm so grateful for all God has given me. Thank You.

I had been attending three to four Alcoholic Anonymous meetings a week since leaving Springbrook, and I was pleased to find a weekly meeting at the Community Center in Scotts Mills. Although there were few women, I felt accepted there. One man who was from Virginia, always ended his discourse in his southern drawl by saying, "I love you and God loves you. Ya'll keep coming back!"

Ron had been on the internet a lot since returning from Romania. In 1996 he struck up a friendship with a woman in one of the popular "Chat Rooms". He returned from some sort of conference in the Midwest in early July and told me he thought we should get a divorce. I had reconsidered the emotional costs and benefits of splitting up with him during his absence and argued that we should try to remain together. We attended a few marital counseling sessions, but the chasm between us was growing. I realized much later that he had met up with his new "friend" at the conference, and that they had most likely had sex.

July 20: Dear Ron, you woke up with that angry "cloud" again. In fact, storm clouds have been brewing for the past day or so. If you must leave me, wait, at least until Jon and Tiff get back from their honeymoon. Also, you needn't leave here. This is your home. I'll go somewhere else. I must be a real drain on you right now. Financially, emotionally…I'm sorry for that.

We began attending the Scotts Mills Friends Church, a Quaker meeting established decades ago by Ron's ancestors. It was small and inviting, but I felt like an outsider.

July 21: I'm sitting in church, alone, feeling stretched, disjointed.…I'm physically drained. Part of me says that this Black and White, Good and Evil Fundamental teaching of the church is the Right Way, that AA is just a "form of Godliness", that I need to lay myself on the altar, confess that I have sinned and unpack all those restraints and restrictions that weigh me down, otherwise I will eventually break under the load. I wish it all were this easy: pray and it will go away. How long has it been since I felt that freedom, the peace that only God can give? So today, my job is to seek God, seek God's will, trust God to work in me. In His time.

In May, Jonathan graduated from George Fox with a degree in Computer Science and he and Tiffany were married in our back yard among the grape arbors on July 26th. It was a simple beautiful ceremony, and I was pleased that my son was happy. Ron took time off from work for several weeks before the wedding to help me paint, prune, and mow. It turned out to be a stressful time for both of us

August 1: Ron finally went to work! It's been a long ten days. God is so good to me. All things work together for good in the long run.

Contact with my brother had been sporadic over the years, and I was pleased when Jane accepted the invitation to come to our home for Mom's birthday celebration.

August 13: Larry, Jane and their kids came last night for a barbeque here at our new home for Mom's birthday! Larry really hugged me. BIG! He initiated it. I am hopeful.

August 23: The last few days have been very difficult for me. Many tears. Ron has a definite anger problem. I told him so last night. He's gone now for four days. I'm a little afraid Sandy, (Kristine's mom) will find me. The phone rang twice, separate times, and no one was there. So now I'm a little afraid.

Life had moved on, but memories of the wreck were never far from my consciousness.

Beth spent the summer working at McDonald's in Newberg and staying out late at night with a group of sketchy individuals. It was time for her to straighten up and get on with her life. She had been accepted to attend George Fox as a freshman, and I had been invited to resume my graduate studies there as well.

September 1: Took Beth to school (George Fox) yesterday. Settled her into her room at George Fox University (The name had been changed from "college" to "university"). She's where she should be. So the house is EMPTY! Ron's gone, Jon's really gone, Beth's gone. Difficult emotions. I'm having mixed feelings about going back to school. I'm looking forward to it but I'm petrified I can't cut it.

September 8: Beth's 18th birthday today. I know that Beth has been (maybe still is) using drugs quite a bit. I need to talk to her, but I don't know how. I returned to school this week.

PART II: THE JOURNALS

1995 - 1999

BEGINNING OF THE END

One cold rainy Fall day our whole family was home, sitting in front of the fire, visiting and laughing. A sense of contentment permeated the home, but I sensed that things would soon change.

September 15: Yesterday was wonderful. The kids (all of them plus Rosie) were there, the fire was glowing, things were quiet, the rain was pouring down.....It was too perfect. I will hold onto that memory for years to come. We were pretending everything was fine. I feel numb toward Ron. I don't know what to think or how to feel.

September 20: Really enjoying school. I don't think I need Ron as much as he needs me. I certainly don't need him for emotional support and that used to be the crux of our relationship. I don't need him to bring wood in or do the lawns because I do it. No wonder I am relieved when he's gone. I really do not think I love him.

October 6: Home alone for the second day. Oh, how I relish my time alone! I'm so confused about how I feel about Ron. So confused. I do not think I can love him as a lover should, as he deserves to be loved. It's not fair. To either of us. He's such a wonderful man. But he drives me nuts! And I enjoy him being gone, can only take him in very small doses.

One crisp October afternoon, Ron and I sat together on the back porch and spoke honestly with one another about our relationship. I told him that I had been wishing he would die, not because I wished him ill, but because I couldn't see growing old with him. He sadly laughed and confessed that he had been having similar thoughts about me. His relationship with Linda, his "Chat Room" friend was getting serious, and I had been flirting with the gentleman from Virginia. Neither of us cared, nor were we jealous. It was time to end our 23-year marriage. I moved in with Rich a few days later.

REBOUND RELATIONSHIP

October 16: Things move fast when they start! We're getting a divorce. I'm living with Rich. We're making love.....a lot. And it's more wonderful than I could've dreamed! Ron and I met today to discuss a settlement. He was going to give me only $10,000. Suzi was there and brought some sense to the conversation. We're going to just split everything in half.

Suzi was my A.A. sponsor and was also my hairdresser. She would be an important source of support and wisdom over the next few years. Suzi advised me that I needed a "new look" and transformed me into a redhead with a bobbed haircut and manicured nails. She was not happy that I had moved in with Rich, advised against having a romantic relationship with another member of A.A., and warned me that it wouldn't end well.

Rich lived in a small ramshackle house situated ten miles up a dirt road on Abiqua Creek near Silverton. It was literally a little cabin in the woods. Rich was an ex-Marine, had several guns, and drove a sturdy pickup. He was charming and a great lover, but very rough on the edges. He was totally opposite from Ron in every way, and I felt safe with him.

October 17: I'm at Rich's right now. I love it here -have been here alone all day. I'm simply happy with Rich. I don't know why. He's a mosaic of simplicity and complexity. So much there that can't be seen. He's not a simple man but he lives a simple honest life. I find myself fascinated with him. It's amazing. And he is a great lover. I anticipate his smile, his touch, and I am stirred within to contemplate such a wonderful event.

My choices during this time of my life continue to mystify me even yet today. Life was tumultuous and I was seeking safety from the storm - swept along by emotions and survival instinct. I made some very unfortunate choices which would haunt me for the rest of my life.

October 26: I'm concerned about sleeping with Rich. I have no guilt. Religious teachings poke their ugly heads out occasionally though as I contemplate my new moral structure. But I am finally being myself, finally feel absolutely blessed by God! How can something so right be wrong? I believe deeply in a loving God who understands human confusions. My life is purer today than it has ever been because I'm being true to myself. I believe in Jesus Christ, but the specifics are fuzzy today. But that is okay.

1997

SECOND THOUGHTS

January 8: So much happens in one month! Divorce is to be final January 19th. Beth almost got kicked out of George Fox for drugs. I moved 99% of my things to Rich's or the storage shed. Now it feels like a serious relationship. It's scary and Rich has gotten real grouchy. I have fears. I long to reunite with God. So far away. I'm searching for the will to live, really live, not just exist up here in the woods.

I was dismayed that no one from church had bothered to contact me after the divorce. Mark Thompson, our pastor from West Chehalem Friends Church had called before I left for Rich's and said, "God hates divorce not because it is sinful but because the process is so hurtful". Otherwise, after almost twenty years of faithful church attendance I was alone.

January 20: I'm seriously questioning my relationship with Rich. Beth is dropping out of Fox, moving in with Jon and Tiff. I am, for now, the family outcast. I feel trapped. Rich is so nasty and grumpy sometimes. He's an emotionally stunted angry man. And it's not fun anymore. I'm not smiling. I feel estranged from all that is important to me: God, my family, Rich. The cat won't even sit on my lap anymore. I think death would be a nice out, but I'm too angry.

February 1: Many questions today: What is sin? And am I living in it? Or am I doing what must be done to stay alive and growing? And is sin what is known only to God for each person? Are these absolutes for behavior, exact rights and wrongs to dictate our very steps? Or is the Spirit of the Law really what I infringe upon when I am not Christ-like? How much of today's "sin" is just stepping on society's popular interpretation of the holy writings of yesterday? What would those writings say if they were written today? I am glad that it is God who judges by what is in my heart and that humankind does not have the ultimate say based on the outward exhibitions of conformance to the heretic demands of others.

Late one evening while gazing at Abiqua Creek from the front porch I had an existential moment of clarity. What had I done? My family was torn apart and I was living with an unprincipled mountain man in the foothills of the Cascade Mountains. I stepped off the porch into the forest and began to walk down the dirt road, screaming and ranting at God and myself. I slumped down next to a stump in the black darkness of a moon-less night, and I sobbed as I contemplated my next move.

April 1: A lot, too much "water under the bridge" since I last wrote. I'm living alone in an apartment in South Salem. So far, It's great. Miss Rich sometimes. Beth went to treatment for twelve days

April 6: Dear God. Here I am. Don't turn away.

May 20: Life is going fairly well except that Beth's life is a mess and I'm trying to keep my hands off.

TEMPORARY "SOLUTION"

I was attending class three days a week, working at the Multnomah County Inverness Jail for my practicum experience, and attending AA meetings three to four times a week. Suzi continued to encourage me and gave me advice as I struggled with mood swings and existential dilemmas. She drove me home from a meeting one night and as she backed out of the driveway, I was filled with a sense of despair and doom. Life was just too difficult, and I was emotionally exhausted.

I unlocked the door to my apartment and impulsively swallowed an entire bottle of Zoloft (an antidepressant).

I immediately regretted my actions and called Suzi who instructed me to go to the Emergency Room. I drove alone to the hospital and was treated with hostility and disgust while a nurse stuck an NG tube down my nose and began the arduous process of pumping my stomach. I sat on the gurney sobbing after the tube was removed and told the discharge nurse how I had, for a moment, succumbed to grief and pain. I told him about my wreck, how I was a nurse, how I had been on my way to care for a patient when the wreck occurred, and that I had impulsively taken the pills. His eyes softened and he spoke softly as he handed me my discharge papers. I do not know why I wasn't referred for counseling and am thankful that I was able to leave the hospital without further ado. I told no one, payed the hospital bill, and buried the horrific memory deep into the recesses of my mind.

June 1: Well that was pathetic! I was in ER last night getting my stomach pumped. No, I will not berate myself. I will learn from this. I forgot God and forgot to pray. How could I? So set on a path of self-sabotage I could/would not see my options. I didn't want to kill myself, just didn't want to feel.

July 20: Today I realize that I must be grateful for the wreck – that defining turning point in my life. Gratitude. It is hard to thank God for pain. But I must surrender. All of me. To God who loves me and wants the best for me. Surrender.

HANGING IN THERE

Ron called in August to tell me he was marrying Linda, his "friend" from the "Chat Room". Beth was a wandering soul, staying with Ron, Jon and Tiff, and friends. She continued to work at McDonald's and had no direction.

September 1: Beth, Oh Beth. Don't know where she's headed. I give her to

God every day. Ron remarried – to Linda. That was hard, but now I feel quite free.

September 9: Beth's birthday was yesterday. She doesn't look like she's doing very well at all. We had a nice day which ended with dinner at Olive Garden with Jon and Tiff, Mom, Beth and me. Beth is living with me for a while which is nice.

September 22: Got Beth settled in her dorm at Central Oregon Community College in Bend today. I feel very good about this whole deal. Very healing weekend with her.

Rich remained in the picture and unfortunately would not entirely disappear for another year. We went to AA meetings, ate out, and, on occasion, had sex. I never had physical chemistry with Ron and had not experienced the intense physical intimacy that I had with Rich. He was a smooth romantic.

One day while walking across campus at George Fox I ran into Jerry Baker, my old pastor from Netarts. We sat together on a bench as I visited with him about the changes in my life. He asked if he could pray for me and we sat holding hands in silence for a few minutes as Quakers are wont to do. He then prayed for me to be healed, content, and to be at peace with myself and God. He was the only Christian who reached out to me during that entire dark journey and I love him for that.

October 15: I feel like a whipped noodle. Didn't feel good about therapy sessions on Monday, gave a crappy presentation today in Faith Development, just wasn't ready and made an ass of myself. I'm tired, I'm fat, I've got a pimple on my nose! Tomorrow will be better. I'm supposed to get my hair colored, and that always makes me feel better about myself. I'm glad I always have the opportunity to change and improve.

I was excelling academically and was working as a psychotherapist at the Student Health Center at Western Oregon State University.

November 28: I have gotten a lot more confident in my role as a professional and have become much more secure in my academic pursuits. I have realized that I will never be, can never be, truly happy with Rich. I told him yesterday (Thanksgiving) that our worlds were too different, that we needed to split for a while. This is it. For good. I know I am a lot more intelligent than him. I am more refined, and those things are very important parts of me. I think he has an "Oppositional Defiant Personality Disorder". So this is it. It is the end. And now I will be the mother I should have been all along, the daughter, the friend, the friend to myself. And maybe now I can really get honest with God.

December 16: Now that I've made my decision, I can see so much about him that I can never live with.

December 30: Rich left a wet Christmas tree on the living room floor, my apartment key on the counter, and took his toothbrush and robe. I saw him on Saturday when I gave him some of his stuff and got the storage shed key. He asked if I wanted to keep dating. Caught me off guard. So...and I'm not proud of this...I said okay.

1998

January 1: I'm ready for a restoration of faith, ready to believe again. It will take a miracle to dissolve the suspicious cynicism and it will take an act of God to erase the blurring line between morality and sin. It may take a lightning bolt to define clearly what a life of integrity would look like for me. What is integrity? I know I didn't have it for a while last year and may not have it now. But I'm getting closer. A year of wondering, of rebellion against myself, God, and the world. "Living in sin". Still smoking, trying half-heartedly to quit.

Mom lived alone in her big house in Mill City. She continued to grieve for my father but refused to seek professional help. I told her she needed to see a counselor, but she replied, "why should I go talk to someone else when I have you?"

January 2: I spent the last few days with Mom. She's repeating herself a lot and she's gotten so old this past year, really lost her spunk.

January 4: Sometimes I feel like I'm in a dream. Here I am, 45, divorced, alone. And Ron is married, comfy in his big farmhouse. Life is not fair. I've made too many mistakes. On one plane my life looks intact, orderly, full of successes. On the other I have failed as a wife, a mother, a friend, and a lover. An old fat woman living alone with her cats doing crossword puzzles and watching TV. Or sitting silently. Just sitting.

Life was full of school, practicum, AA meetings and sporadic visits with my children. I felt positive about my future and, on occasion, I enjoyed a sense of peace and contentment.

January 27: A new life – a new beginning – Hope rings out, Rays of wholesome health ripple through my being – Excitement – Zeal – Anticipation – to Live, to Feel – to Bathe in all God so lovingly and wisely and patiently endows. Life is worth living today. Today stretches before me – already tiny smudges and toe prints decorate the path….the shroud is lifted. The sun shines – glows warmly. I am a child of God.

Ron called one afternoon and asked "do you think we tried hard enough to keep our marriage together? Did we do the right thing?" I suspected that his second marriage was not turning out to be all he had hoped it would be. "Ron, we can't have this conversation. You're married and that's that" I replied.

April 5: Disturbing dreams, feeling unsettled, stressed. Second-guessing my past decisions. Blaming myself for all the pain inflicted on my family, feeling alone. So alone. And wishing I could go back and fix it all. But Ron remarried. I wonder if he has regrets.

A REALLY BAD IDEA

I received $25,000 in the divorce settlement and needed to reinvest in property in order to avoid paying an excess in taxes. I was, on occasion, still seeing Rich who offered me the opportunity to purchase a place on the Abiqua Creek. He promised me "you'll get your money back Phyllis, I promise. I'm always good for my word."

He had remained in my life and, like a piece of gum stuck to the bottom of my shoe, was difficult to dislodge.

June 1: Rich and I are buying a place together. It is the perfect home for me. Dear God, fill me up with good things today. Allow me to shine brightly into the lives of others.

July 3: I fear I have made a mistake: I am aligned with a man who I do not love, stuck with this relationship because of the house.

July 20: I trust, O God that when I can only believe in the simplest of truths and find myself unable to accept the Christo-centric ways of others, that you will hold me close, and shield me from evil.
I trust you will be patient with my questioning, my painful withdrawal from all I once embraced as truth.
I seek your face and thirst after truth. Remove the cynical doubt and replace it with honest pursuit of truth.

July 28: I know I must end my romantic relationship with Rich. I know that deep within.

July 30: Hope is engendered by the simple glimmer of belief that God has not given up on me.

August 6: *I realize now how guilt has directed my choices, causing me to settle for second best, resign myself to the mundane. Tried to break up with Rich. He is quite persistent. So for now we're "cooling" our relationship for a few months. I think I will simply ask for my part of the money and leave, hopefully not before Christmas.*

August 14: I got all my stuff from Rich's today (and took his stuff up). I told Rich I was breaking up with him. He is understandably angry and hurt. Feeling remorse and regret for the past, choosing Rich. He's gone now, essentially out of my life. I'm allowing myself to see his faults, to admit to the persistent dishonest and secretiveness that I cannot live with.

Beth returned from an academically unsuccessful year at the

community college in Bend, moved in with me, and began working at an Adult Foster Home for mentally disabled adults. Jon was succeeding as a computer programmer while Tiffany attended college at Linfield College. My children were especially happy that I was rid of Rich. They did not care for him at all. I began to attend Silverton Friends Church and, on occasion, played the piano for the worship service.

September 8: It's amazing to think that exactly 20 years ago to this moment I had just given birth to Beth. What a gift she has been. I love her so much and am so happy we are in each other's lives once again! Thankyou God!

I had not spoken to my brother since the divorce and, although I lived only one mile from him when I lived in Salem, he and Jane had not reached out to me. They knew that I was divorced and was living alone but I had not received so much as phone call from them. His son David was to be married in Scio and Mom asked me to accompany her to the wedding.

September 19: Going to David's wedding today. I get to see the enemy.

September 20: Got through the wedding. So superficial, meeting the "family". Larry was warm, distant, strained. Why? I would like a family too.

REVOLVING DOOR

Rich knocked on my door and charmed me back into his life.

October 10: Hypocrite. I had sex with the man that I do not love. That is usually called a sin. This morning he came over and we both knew why, there was no pretending. And I feel very badly about it. Slut. Whore. How can I be true to myself now? If there's a God in heaven, and I know there is, things will have to work out. My sense of who I am is all muddled. I don't know anymore. Lonely. Feeling weak, vulnerable.

October 18: My life is getting convoluted. I'm playing for church today. I made love with someone I'm not committed to yesterday. I'm aspiring to be a morally conscious psychologist. Can I live with the tension and contradiction? And who am I dragging along with me down this road of chaos?

Memories of the wreck and ensuing turmoil continued to seep into my thoughts and subconsciousness.

November 8: I cannot avoid knowing what day this is. Seven years ago, my life turned upside down. Still plagued, haunted. Still so afraid of bumping into someone who knows or is the family. The pain has forced me to grow, to reformulate my belief system, to totally disassemble my world in order for me to build it back up again. Slowly, piece by piece. The blocks are still being reconstructed. Each block has its own form and essence and sometimes resembles those that once formed my life.

Rich still wouldn't go away.

December: Whenever I have gone a few days without Rich around I feel so free. I'm praying for God to release me from him somehow, maybe by giving me the strength to confront. I realize that fear is underlying my choices regarding Rich. If I didn't live here, I would surely be rid of him entirely. It seems like a bad dream sometimes, this continued tryst-like relationship with Rich. Secretive. Never in public. It's so unfair to both of us.

December 26: All alone. I did it again. So lonely last night and let Rich stay over. I am so weak. Sometimes I feel like giving up. So, I ask God, once again, for forgiveness.

PREPARING TO LEAVE

Beth was living with me and told me that I was in an "abusive relationship" with Rich. I was in my fourth year of graduate school, and l and had begun to apply for the mandatory year-long psychology internship for the following year. My hope was that I would be accepted to a Veterans Affairs (V.A.) hospital where I would have opportunities to work with older adults. I applied to eighteen sites, and I took out a small loan to fund plane trips and lodging for interviews in Colorado, Texas, South Dakota, and Iowa.

137

1999

I told Rich that I could not see him anymore, and that I was officially discontinuing the relationship. He was angry and became sullen and spiteful. One afternoon I smelled something and looked out the window to see Rich spreading manure all over the front lawn. I objected saying the lawn did not need to be tended to. Rich sneered that he was still "the owner" and had a right to fertilize the lawn. One week later he delivered a cord of wet wood, an overt act of spite. Dry wood would really have been nice (I heated our home exclusively with a wood stove and bought all my wood from Rich for $100/cord). I began to be afraid of him.

January 31: Sitting in church. Wish things were as simple as I once thought they were. I would like to believe completely, would like to forge ahead, living a life of purity. He's coming over today. I know he is.

February 17: God is still protecting me from Rich. It's been a while since I saw him. It's a great relief to be untangled.

The fourth-year psychology graduate students around the country were notified of their internship placements at the same time on the same day: February 22, 8:00 Pacific Standard Time. I waited breathlessly at the computer awaiting to see if, or where, I would be moving for the next year.

February 22: I'm going to Iowa! I'm so excited and know this is just as it's supposed to be!

Because I had decided I wanted no more to do with the property, Rich and I drew up some papers establishing his obligation to pay me my portion of the investment ($22,000). I rode with him in his pickup to a local bank to get the paper notarized. As we turned up the road towards my home, I feared that he would drive up into the woods and he would kill me.

February 27: What a week. First, I get the internship site of my dreams.

Next, Rich rails on me for "using" him for 2 ½ years.   I spent all Tuesday interviewing inmates for my dissertation. Then yesterday Sam, my patient, hangs himself. In the middle I have wreck dreams.

WE NEED TO MOVE. AGAIN.

March 8: Rich was back to his nasty self yesterday. I must leave

March 16: Rich hasn't been around for days. I am worried about my safety.

I returned from class one day to find a note waiting for me on the kitchen counter. "This world will be a better place when you're gone". Beth and I needed to move to Mom's, but first we had to find a home for our dear dog Jude. One cold rainy Saturday, Beth took him to a man I had met while working at the jail, who had offered to take him.

March 19: Yesterday was a dreadfully hard day. Jude is gone.   I cried all morning. Rich showed up. Mean, vile, accusatory, vindictive, sucking me into a place of despair and self-hate. Now battling remorse and regret.

 I called the pastor of the Silverton Friends Church, Ron Woodward, and explained the situation.   I asked for assistance with moving my belongings to a storage shed.   He and two other men from the church drove to my house early the next day, helped me pack the house, and we filled my storage unit in Silverton.   Beth and I were free.

March 23: Settled at Mom's. I think this will be a very good thing. She needs me too.

March 24: I am so happy today! This is a new day full of hope and promise. God has been so faithful to protect me through all this in spite of myself. God has a plan for me – many plans. And He has never given up on me, although I often gave up on Him/Her.

March 27: I'm very thankful to be here, to be away from Rich. The farther away (timewise) I get, the clearer it is that I was so very insane to ever be with him!

How could I? I must not beat up on myself.

I had been employing the very efficient defense mechanism of denial ever since my first days with Rich. He received his mail at the post office, and usually ripped it up as soon as he read the return address. He forbade me to listen to his phone messages, however, when he was gone, I turned on the answering machine to hear demands from collection agencies and the voice of Christy, a young woman I had met at AA. She called multiple times to plea with him to acknowledge that he was the father of her baby. When questioned, Rich denied any prior involvement with her, and I accepted his words as truth, although, a pervasive sense of distrust and doubt gnawed at my justification for continuing a relationship with him.

I sought legal counsel (about a year after I moved to Iowa) with hopes of receiving my $22,000 back from Rich. My attorney tracked him down and found that He was married and had another child. Within another year, his wife was pregnant again and he moved away to hide in the Mountains of Montana. I never got my money back.

LEAVING MOM AND BETH

Beth began attending class at Chemeketa Community College, and I was working at the Linn County Community Mental Health Center for my final practicum experience. One morning I was headed down the road from Mom's to Albany when I had a strong urge to turn the car around. Upon my return home, I found Mom lying unconscious on the floor.

March 30: Mom's in the hospital with pneumonia.

April 1: Mom is home, very weak. Life is good, full, peaceful. I'm so grateful! Beth got all A's and one B. I'm so proud! Jon is doing so well. All the loved ones in my life are being well taken care of. And I'm at peace for once. Hope and peace.

April 2: Larry called and chewed her out for not telling him she was sick etc.

Now I'm fighting resentment toward him and his "darling" family.

I was relieved to be at Mom's, and I began to attend local Alcoholics Anonymous meetings close to her home; however, intrusive thoughts and existential reckoning had become a common thread in my life.

April 17: Dreams dreams dreams… Reconciliation with Ron dreams. Struggling with the two person dilemma: Who I am and who I appear to be (in my dream), realizing I would have to sacrifice the real (rebellious, cynical, sensual, sexual) for the façade (compliant, obedient, sterile) if I reunited with Ron.

April 19: Spent the day with Deedra (a friend from AA). She said that I had more "class" in my little finger than Rich has in his whole body.

April 28: I can't believe I've completed four years of school (over a 5- year period). The beginning seems like a year ago and a decade ago.

Beth continued to attend school, and would periodically stay with her father, but not all was well in her life.

April 30: I drove over to see Beth at Ron's. He wasn't home and she was in a puddle of tears, sitting on the kitchen floor. So depressed! I got her in to see her shrink and then a nurse practitioner for medication. She has Major Depression and was put on Prozac. My sweet Beth. Like mother, like daughter. I ache for her.

May 16: Playing piano at Silverton Friends today. "Be still and know that I am God". (God whispers to me in my comfort and screams to me in my pain). "I love you and have great things in store for you".

May 27: Mom fell again during the night going to the bathroom. Falling frequently now. She asks a lot of questions but doesn't listen to the answers, especially if she doesn't like the answers. So, I spoke with her about handrails, more phones, getting a Life-Line unit. I know Mom will not do well living alone after I leave. I'm feeling sad, angry, helpless. Can't make her do anything. I never realized how stubborn she is. I'm leaving in a little more than a month and these things must be resolved.

141

The reality was that Mom was in the very early stages of vascular dementia. I begged for her to move to Iowa with me, but she refused. She loved sharing coffee with her past students and old friends, who dropped by to visit. She wanted to live out her days in her own home. When I suggested that she use a cane or a walker, she argued, "those are for old people". She was 79 years old when I left for Iowa.

June 12: Spent the entire day with Beth yesterday. What a wonderful bonding time! We hiked the perimeter of Silver Creek Falls (ten miles!). I am so encouraged about her future. She has such insight and direction now. I'm hopeful that her life will now begin to blossom and that she will experience the joy and excitement of life right now!

June 27: I'm feeling better about Mom. She'll do okay. It will all be okay.

My brother's son had a new baby. Mom wanted me to take her there to see him for a visit before I left for Iowa. My brother and Jane were also there, and as we prepared to leave for home, I pulled him aside and asked him to call or check in on Mom at least once a week while I was in Iowa. He replied, "I won't be able to do that. I go to Europe a lot. Sorry." Oh, they don't have phones in Europe?

Jon, Beth, Tiffany and I loaded up a Ryder Truck with all my earthly belongings on June 30. Jonathan had insisted on moving me to Iowa, and after attending my last day of class on July 1st, I hopped in the truck and we headed down the highway to Iowa. I thought I was leaving Oregon for one year.

PART III: THE JOURNALS

1999 - 2002

IOWA

Jon and I drove into Knoxville, Iowa on what turned out to be the hottest day that year. It was hot all day and all night. I was accustomed to Oregon, where one can expect things to cool off at night, but it was still 100 degrees at midnight. I had rented a small house, and a few of my new colleagues helped us unload the truck.

July 3: Iowa. Hot, muggy. We made it! Long trip. Jon has moved me in with help from my new colleagues. Feeling overwhelmed, emotionally fragile. Need to cry.

July 4: Home alone. Alone for the first time since I moved in with Mom. I must remember that God has not brought me this far just to drop me on my head!

I reported to my first day of work on July 5th. I joined the two other interns, Tim and Paul, as we were given a tour of the V.A. facility. I was alarmed when we were shown tree stumps left over from the "last tornado". I hadn't done any research about this distant land and (unbeknownst to me) I would ride out many tornado warnings over the ensuing years in shelters and basements.

We were to enjoy a full year working with, and being supervised by, eight well-seasoned psychologists. In one year, I would leave with the confidence and expertise needed to blossom into a full-fledged psychologist. I would like to give a special thank you to David Dettman, Ph.D., Mike Gaffney, Ph.D., Tomas Gonzeles, Ph.D. and my primary supervisor Bob Hutzell Ph.D. for giving me a stellar internship experience.

July 8: Knoxville Iowa – a friendly town in a hot humid state. My two fellow interns, Paul and Tim, are really nice and I think we're going to be a good team. I actually like my little house now. It's cute! I think I'll be happy here. This house is where I am supposed to be. Making friends at AA.

July 15: I have started my rotation full force with Bob. That has given me a sense of direction that I haven't had for a while. The loneliness has lifted for

145

today. I'm getting focused on the task at hand and am enthused about my job. Life is beginning to take on a bit of a routine.

I worked all day, attended AA meetings twice a week, worked on my dissertation and began to get my rental home in order. But the world had not stopped turning back in Oregon.

July 22: Started the day in tears. Just getting to sleep and Mom calls. Then just getting to sleep again and Roseanne calls to tell me Mom is falling all over the place and I need to call the doctor. (Mom says she's "fine"). And Beth broke up with Eli and I'm so afraid she's gay.

I called the Department of Human Services in Oregon and asked them to assess whether my mother was safe living alone in her home. They had made an appointment to see her, and to prepare for their arrival, Mother baked chocolate chip cookies and had a hot pot of coffee ready when they knocked on the door. They called me a week later to tell me she was "just fine".

July 23: Called Beth and asked her straight out. She thinks she's gay. I've always wondered. My heart is so heavy...I do not want that for my baby girl.

I was not opposed to my daughter being gay. I had, however, counseled several young lesbians at the Western Oregon State University Student Health Center as they dealt with depression and suicidal ideation. I knew that, even in 1999, my daughter would run into obstacles and resistance as she continued to navigate through her life.

August 18: I called back home tonight. Not so good. Beth's car broke down. Mom was in a dither again.

STEVE

Steve was a social worker at the Knoxville V.A., and I met him on my first day of orientation in the Day Treatment Center. He was about the same age as the other veterans in the room, and, at first, I thought he was a patient. Eventually I realized that he was the facilitator of the mental health group we had come to observe. Later he would ask me "didn't you notice my name tag?". I found out that the first time he saw me he thought to himself: "there's someone I could be married to".

Steve was the third of four boys who had all worked for their father's construction business from very young ages. He attended college after high school, partly to avoid the draft, and partly because he didn't want to be a construction worker for the rest of his life. A letter from Uncle Sam was waiting for him the day he returned home after completing his Bachelor of Science in sociology. He was drafted into the Army in June of 1972 and served for two years as a counselor at an Army clinic in Georgia for returning soldiers who had become addicted to drugs or alcohol. He then used the GI bill to return to University of Iowa for a Master of Social Work degree and later attained a Master of Science Degree in Health Care Administration. He was a single parent to his 13-year-old son, owned his home, and had a convertible and a pickup. He was quite a catch!

August 4: I met a nice man at work. Really nice (Steve). I'll look back on this entry someday and smile about how silly it is to have been drawn to him, or I will be amused because I will have gotten to know him and realized it wasn't at all a good fit, or I'll realize that this entry was the beginning of something.

August 14: Steve expressed an intent to date. Actually, I took a risk and invited him to go to the races with Tim, Paul, and Laura. But he's going on vacation, so we'll have to wait a week.

August 22: Had a date with Steve on Friday! Going on a picnic with him today. Calls from home not good. Mom's getting progressively senile.

August 26: Steve is really expressing a lot of interest. I'm obsessing, my mind filled with sexual fantasy. I wonder if I'm just lonely and longing for a man's physical touch – to be held and loved. Dream last night: Rich was at my door with a gun.

August 29: Nice dinner at a fancy restaurant with Steve last night then drove for a while. Then....Oh my goodness! To my house to "look for bats" which ended in about three hours of torrid lovemaking. I still feel weak-kneed thinking about it. He's so good in bed! I just enjoyed Steve the whole night – all of it. He is not at all like a man I am normally drawn to. No red flags at all. He's a gentle, kind, slightly OCD man who cares greatly for his son. He's short, very put together, very responsible, intelligent.

NO LONGER ANONYMOUS

Doctor Gaffney asked to see me one day during work, and as I sat across the desk from him, I worried that something was wrong. He was usually laid back with an easy smile, but today he looked very serious. He had received a complaint from one of the outpatient mental health veterans that I was "spying" on him at AA meetings. Let's review what AA stands for: "Alcoholics ANONYMOUS". My anonymity suddenly went out the window. I attended a few out-of-town AA meetings after that. I eventually quit going to AA entirely a few weeks after I met Steve.

ADJUSTMENT

September 4: Good chat with Jon last night. Feeling hopeful, a little scared, but mostly in a chronic state of subdued excitement. Steve has brought a new dimension into my life. The one piece that's omitted is church. Still need to fit that in, somehow. But God is here, blessing me, blessing my relationship with Steve somehow. There's a goodness and a sort of purity between us.

I tried to call Mom almost every day, and although she assured me that she was fine, I was skeptical. Beth was settling in at George Fox and everything seemed right in the world for Jonathan and Tiffany.

September 7: Good talk with Beth last night. She is doing well at George Fox. Realizing that I need to tend to Mom's needs over my own wants to be with Steve. Can't just stay in Iowa and leave Mom alone. I think I am going to be with Steve the rest of my life.

September13: Jon turned twenty-five yesterday. I'm so proud and I love him so much.

Steve and I were seeing each other every day, and I had started staying with him on the weekends. His 13-year-old son Kent had returned from visiting his mom in Florida, and I admired Steve because he was obviously doing a great job being a single parent to his son. Kent was accepting of this new lady in his home and continued to be loving and kind to me even when he and his father were at odds. Steve shared with me that he realized he was an alcoholic when Kent was a toddler. He had attended outpatient substance abuse treatment; however, he had not felt the need to go to AA. He had not had a drink of alcohol for twelve years.

September 15: I am so in love it hurts. The passion, the distraction. The only problem with Steve is his lack of spiritual life. But he does believe, not in a religion though. He has thrown his life into parenting for the past ten years and I think is ready to really live and experience life. He says that some very big holes in his life have been filled up with me in his life.

September 23: I've never loved anyone this much and It's so hard.

Things seemed to be calming down back in Oregon. Mom had hired a house cleaner and another woman was coming in weekly to assist her when she took a bath or shower.

September 29: Great phone call with Mom last night – she's doing well.

October 6: Everything in my life appears to be in order. That is a strange occurrence for me. When I examine every aspect I can see that each piece is falling into place and that ultimately all is going well. I love a man who loves me, my job is good, my health is okay, I have friends, news from back home is relatively free of crisis at this moment. I feel loved by many, hated by none. What more can I ask of God and life? I am so inured to chaos that this feels odd.

October10: Steve continues to be so....perfect? No, but maybe perfect for me. God is blessing me so much I could cry.

I was not attending church but continued to pray and read devotionals every morning.

October 21: Sometimes the futility of life crashes in on my serenity and seems to tear it apart. How could I ever manage this life without God in my life? This God who loves me so much, who gives me strength and guidance for each day. Is religion just a human invention? Our attempt to understand, to make sense of things? Religion aside, I know that my God is real.

Mom called to explain that her television was "broken", and that she had called Larry, who lived only thirty minutes away. He replied that he was "too busy" to assist her. She subsequently called Ron, and within a few days Ron had purchased and installed a new television. Mom voiced a great deal of disappointment with Larry but was relieved to know she could depend on Ron for assistance. I called Ron to thank him and he said, "I told your dad I would always be there to take care of your mom and I'm keeping my promise to him".

October 22: Call with Ron and Beth last night. Ron is helping Mom get set up with assistance in the home. I so appreciate that. We need Rons in the world, I think.

November 1: I've been contemplating theological questions and am at peace right now to just accept God's love. I don't have to know right now. I do know God is directing, that God is in charge. God knows I believed fiercely in the Christian way before the wreck, and that it was not of my own doing that terrible day. So in that I am shielded and will continue to strive for purpose and sense in it all. I'm drawn to the notion of a loving Christ as well, do not feel condemned but very much loved.

November 4: God stuff. Too hard to contemplate right now, but I believe God is smiling on us right now, smiling on me, loving me, protecting me. He/She brought Steve into my life for a reason, a good reason. Love is too strong to deny. Now and then I feel as if my heart will burst. He holds me so tight, so close...He loves me so much too. This must last.

FIRST YEAR IN IOWA

I returned to Oregon for a week in November to spend Thanksgiving with my family. Mom appeared to be marginally safe: She had frequent visitors, "Meals on Wheels", a Life-Line unit, a house cleaner, and a Nursing Assistant who came three times a week to assist with personal care. Beth appeared to be managing well at college and Jon and Tiffany were their usual responsible selves.

November 21: Beth, Jon, and Tiff picked me up from the airport. They're all doing well, even Beth who is talking about a boyfriend! Mom.....not vastly different from when I left. I'm not sure what else she needs to be safe here, nor do I know if she can be convinced to change anything. And she's still driving some. That's scary!

November 22: Rough talk with Mom and now I'm doubting how bad she is. She does seem to be improving some. Maybe she'll be okay. I do enjoy seeing my kids and seeing Mom. But this isn't where I belong now.

Beth came to visit me in Iowa during Christmas break. She had lost weight and was somewhat unkempt. She assured me that she was doing "okay" in school and that all was well in her life.

December 24: Beth asleep, Kent asleep....Life is good today. Spent yesterday Christmas baking with Beth at my house. God has me right where I'm supposed to be.

2000

January 2: I moved a lot of my stuff over to Steve's and am settling in. Life is very good today. The contentment I feel is akin to that of my early childhood. I never thought this could be possible again.

January 6: Life is so full, and God is giving me the opportunity to positively impact the life of others. Beth has been suspended from George Fox (for drugs?) so I guess she's starting all over again.

I returned to Oregon multiple times during the next few months to receive assistance with my dissertation from my advisor and the statistics professor. My dissertation explored correlations between childhood sexual abuse and alcohol abuse and was based on 100 structured interviews with female inmates at the Multnomah County Inverness Jail. I always stayed with Mom when I returned to Oregon.

February 20: Here I am at Mom's longing desperately to go home. When I'm here the memories are more acute, and I ponder more deeply things that should be tabled for now. Theology of Salvation – Hell, Heaven, Right, Wrong. I never could fully accept, even before the wreck. I always knew, at my core, that the urgency of guilt – that persistent gnawing of uncertainty – was not true. I could and can accept the loving god and concede that there is a line between good and evil. But only God knows that line for it differs within each heart and soul. Are we all given a second chance? I am not evil, for I seek God's face daily. I would believe traditional Christian thought if I could, but I can't. Am I a Christian? I believe that Jesus did come to show us the way of peace and reconciliation. I do believe that God is personal and here. Forgiving sins? We are all human and will err, will make mistakes. I guess the notion of sin catches me, baffles me. I'm asking for God's guidance and direction each day. I have always loved God. Always. I wish I could believe in the simple black and white. I cannot.

THIS IS SERIOUS

Life with Steve took on a nice rhythm. I worked during the weekdays and wrote on my dissertation during the evenings and weekends. Steve and I took long drives, attended concerts and enjoyed getting to know one another. I was desperately in love with him and could not envision living the remainder of my life without him.

April 1: Steve gave me a one carat ring yesterday after work, on the couch, with the classic rock station playing. Sweet man. He had picked it up in the afternoon and just couldn't wait to give it to me!

April: 16: It's Easter time and I want to go to church, but I don't want to be confounded further. I miss church but what really does it represent for me now? I miss the music, the corporate prayer. Something is missing now. I know that no matter how confused I may be, no matter what theological questions linger, I can still make a difference in the world today.

Beth had dropped out of college again, was working at a sandwich shop in Newberg, and had begun dating Nate, a young man from George Fox.

April 19: Beth's engaged to be married. Not pregnant, wants to get married this summer. She sounds so happy so I'm happy for her!

GRADUATION

Steve and I flew out to Oregon a few days before my graduation and were able to spend meaningful time with my mother, daughter, son, and daughter-in-law. My family warmly accepted Steve and one afternoon we were visiting Mom when she began talking about some of her close friends. She described them as "not normal" because they were vegetarians, they attended the Unitarian Church, their daughter travelled around Europe for a year before starting college, and they received acupuncture for their aches and pains. I thought they sounded like very interesting people, and said as much, but Mom argued "but they're not normal". I asked, "what is normal, Mom?" She sat back in her chair and smiled, "we're normal Honey, we're normal". That explained a lot.

My hooding ceremony and graduation were the happiest events of my life.

April 28: I gave a brief speech at the Hooding Ceremony today. I spoke about Viktor Frankl and how the Search for Meaning is the primary motivation in each person's life. "Life can only be understood backward but it must be lived forward" (Kierkegaard). God does not waste pain. Suffering softens us, helps us to feel more compassion and love toward one another. Our sense of belonging to the human race, our recognition of the interdependence and kinship of us all, are the most cherished result of the gift of pain. Life is a journey, and this is a happy ending to a sad story. I ask every day, "What can I give to this day?" And I pray that I will give more to my fellows than I take away.

Jon and Tiffany held a graduation party for me the next day after the formal graduation ceremony. Thirty-five friends and family members came to the celebration.

May 7: I am awed that I am a doctor. I must be careful not to feel prideful or "better-than". I am actually humbled. But sometimes I want to say "Don't you know? I'm a doctor!" to no one in particular. Beth is doing well, Jon is happy, and Mom is okay. They live in their worlds, I have mine. As it should be.

BACK HOME

We returned to our home in Knoxville, and I began to pursue the post-graduate placement required before I could take my national psychology board exam to become a licensed psychologist for the State of Iowa. I was hired as a full-time psychologist by Iowa Veterans Home in Marshalltown, Iowa and I would not be returning to Oregon to live any time soon.

May 28: My mind is noisy with contorted images from the past. Mostly disturbing and unsettling with themes of regret, remorse, and disgust at past behaviors and decisions. My former life was so long ago. It's so distant, like a dream. And so the present is like a dream-state, surreal....how did I get here, who am I, where am I? Life is good. My love for Steve grows and I'm living in a totally new dimension. A dimension without God? No. Oh absolutely No. But a dimension without/lacking religion, a proscribed form of approaching God. This dimension is lacking the structure I once had, the structure of guilt, expectations, shame. Now the structure is of a natural makeup of rhythm, desires, logical sequence, no extreme high and low. No crisis. Just a plodding along, putting one foot ahead of the other.

June 4: I have struggled for a while now to align my inner with my outer. The strong woman vs. weak woman; the best vs. the worst. But I am a combination, and not a combination of bad and good. Rather a diverse collage of abilities and strengths. I will not give up. I choose to live.

July 1: Last day of Internship. I'm a doctor.

I had completed all academic and experiential requirements and had earned the degree of Doctorate of Psychology (Psy.D.) from George Fox University.

Some stories would end right here. She survived and achieved her dream. But it has been two decades since I earned my doctorate. Life goes on, along with the joys and pain of breathing......of simply being. I used to think that when one achieved a certain age, certain milestones, life would just smooth out. There would be no heartache, no strife. Everything would fit into place. It turns out I was wrong.

DOCTOR PHYL

July 9: First day of work at Iowa Veteran's Home. I think I'll really enjoy this job. Staff is positive, fun.

July 16: Deep within a dark space begins to grow and threatens to engulf my soul. But I resist, thrashing back with rational reasoning. Steve seems to think that I should be able to combat the demons with intellect, with self-imposed cognitive reframing. Because I'm a psychologist. I should be able to cure myself, to quell the fear, the anger, the insanity. A darkness persists and often envelops me. But no tears can fall. There may be no more. Steve does not, cannot understand the pain, the guarding, the tension of evil and good. I should be happy. I should be.

August 6: Do other people go through life with this kind and amount of angst? Nice routine at home. Steve – comfortable, loving. The angst has lifted for now. Perhaps my needs are met by giving to others at work. Giving is so therapeutic.

WINE and a WEDDING

Beth and Nate were to be married in August in Ron's back yard. My flight to Portland was cancelled but United Airlines was able to find me another flight on Delta Airlines where I was seated in first class for the first time in my life. As the plane taxied down the runway, I was handed my first free glass of wine. Beth met me several hours later at the gate and I was drunk. I vomited into a waste basket as we walked to her car. We headed toward her apartment to make final wedding plans. A few days after arriving in Oregon I called my AA sponsor Suzi who said, "get your butt to a meeting". At her direction I went to one AA meeting in Salem and that was the last AA meeting I ever attended.

August 24: Mom's bedroom smells like urine. I'm smoking again. Feeling so stressed. I want to go home and pretend it's all okay.

September 1: Got through the wedding. Beth was beautiful wearing a wreath of flowers in her hair and barefoot! Great to see all the ex in-laws. Mom did okay.

Upon my return to Iowa, Steve and I sat on the patio as I told him that I had allowed myself to get drunk. He was incredulous and didn't understand how I could be so careless. But then, this was a man who had just decided to quit drinking one day and never had a problem since then. This was also a man who quit smoking "cold turkey" one day because it wasn't good for him. He didn't understand, and I'm not sure I did either.

September 22: Emotionally pretty stable. Had a weird panic attack this week. Don't know why. Wreck thoughts occasionally intrude these days. Maybe It's because of Fall.

October 8: Went to church at College View Friends in Oskaloosa. "Preach always and if necessary, use words".

November 23: Believing in the loving, caring, all-knowing Jesus will be something I must always do, can't help but do, like breathing.

A SIMPLE UNION

We were married in Steve's living room on December 1st. The wedding party included Mark Minear, a fellow psychologist and a

Quaker minister; Tim Wahl my "bridesmaid" and former fellow intern; his fiancé Deanna; and of course Steve's 14 year-old son Kent (who forgot to put shoes on and stood in his socks throughout the ceremony).

December 2: Our wedding yesterday was beautiful, simple and sweet, meaningful, intimate. I sang "Grow Old Along with Me" to Steve. Wow. We're married! And I'm so happy! Truly in love, loving…..

December 9: The only thing certain in life is that nothing ever stays the same.

December 24: Christmas Eve. Steve went to candlelight service with me. I called Mom this evening. She shared some disturbing content about a conversation she had with Jane. I am just seething with the desire to tell her (Jane) off. I feel like writing my whole brother's family off. Just erasing them. All they've brought is hurt.

I had lived in Knoxville for over a year and began to feel homesick, especially for my family.

December 30: Sometimes I feel that my heart may break in two. I may just be grieving. This may be "normal". But oh, how I miss my kids, my mom, my family. And yes, I miss Ron in a way that is hard to describe. I wouldn't want to be married to him, but I miss the companionship, the knowing, the comfort. Those things I have yet to develop fully with Steve: That very relaxed "knowing" of each other, the reading of minds, the knowing of physical expression, not needing words.

2001

January 29: A poignant dream last night. An Earth-mother asked me what sign I was. At first I didn't want to tell her, but then I said "Scorpio". "Ah" she replied, "then you must be a person whose life's meaning is in helping others".

IOWA VETERANS HOME

Iowa Veterans Home housed about 800 residents comprised of veterans of all ages and their spouses in several long-term care units.

Homeless and/or chronically mentally ill (but physically independent) veterans resided in the Domiciliary - a large old building set apart from the rest of the facility. Healthy spouses of veterans being cared for in the Alzheimer's unit also lived there. I provided psychotherapy and assessment services to patients in my cozy office as well as at the bedside of residents in the nursing units. I consulted with nursing staff regarding behavioral issues and began teaching in-services for medical staff throughout the facility. Some days I would sit in my office chair and think "I'm being paid for this! I would do this for free!" I began to receive invitations from outside entities to speak on a variety of topics and I would eventually provide trainings at regional, state, and national conferences and trainings.

My office was easily accessible to the residents. One day a woman knocked on my office door and asked if I could help her with a problem. She was about 80 years old and lived in the Domiciliary while her demented husband of 50 years resided in the Alzheimer's unit. I invited her to join me and she said, "I've got a big problem. I'm in love for the first time in my life". She described a life of being physically and mentally abused by her husband and went on to explain that she had never loved her husband. She had, however, met an older single gentleman at the facility and had fallen in love with him. She explained that they spent hours together playing cards and taking walks and how she felt young and vibrant when she was with him. She was a devout Christian and believed that it would be a sin to leave her husband. But more importantly, she would no longer be able to live at Iowa Veterans Home if she divorced her husband. There really was no easy solution to her dilemma, but I continued to see her regularly for encouragement and guidance throughout the next year. Her boyfriend died the following year and I met with her for a while after that for grief counseling.

In April, Tim Wahl and I took the national psychology exam together in Des Moines and both of us passed. I passed by two points, but I passed (psychology joke: What do you call a person who barely passes the national psychology exam? Answer: A psychologist). We took our state oral exams in the Fall and became officially licensed clinical psychologists for the state of Iowa. Tim went on to have a successful career in his private practice in Knoxville and continues to be one of my dearest friends.

I continued to worry about Mother as time passed. I offered to take an extended absence from my job so that I could move back to Oregon and live with her and, hopefully, assist her with a move to a safer environment. She wouldn't hear of it and said, "if you come back, I'm writing you out of my will! I will disown you!"

May 5: Saw Tower of Power last night at Val Air Ballroom. Came home to find four phone messages about Mom who is confused due to a bladder infection. Jane was verbally involved, Ron is actively involved, and things are covered for now, with Beth coming to help her along with neighbors. May be a stroke. Awoke with very negative thoughts of Jane on my mind.

May 25: I passed the national psychology exam!

Maybe Dad had been wrong about me being "cute but not very smart".

MUSIC AND BICYCLES

Steve was a "Roadie" for a rock band ("Children of Darkness" from Oskaloosa Iowa) when he was in high school. He had spent much of his younger life listening to albums and attending concerts. He had seen Janis Joplin, Creedence Clearwater, Cream, Steppin' Wolf, The Grateful Dead and The Doors live in concert, while I had been changing diapers and listening to the local radio station in Tillamook. The sounds of Jazz and the Blues echoed through our home in Knoxville. On the weekends we attended concerts and sipped Sprite in Blues Bars.

May 28: Went to a Delbert McClinton concert last night. It was very good! I enjoy getting to see and know this dimension of life – the music-makers, the other

159

side, where the beat and the pulse and the rhythm draw us in and represent the heart of our beings, the passion of the pulse. Sometimes it's as if I just crawled out from under a rock!

We were riding bikes every weekend and logged almost 800 miles that summer. I felt physically healthy and pleased to be in such a wholesome relationship. On September 11th, I was leaving my office to facilitate a group and our secretary Sue said a plane had just crashed in New York City. I stood in the Rec Room with other staff and residents as we watched a second plane hit a building, and I cried as the buildings crumbled to the ground.

A NATION IN GRIEF

September 15: Tragedy hit our nation this week: four hijacked planes – two hit the World Trade Center, one hit the Pentagon, and the fourth crashed in rural Pennsylvania. We are under terrorist attack. Who knows what will unfold?

September 23: Our nation is getting "back to normal" but will never regain the same sense of security. Some seem so caught off guard, taken aback: How can this happen in the U.S.? Others have long expected this sort of event. We didn't know when, who, what, or how, but we knew that the arrogant complacency of Americans would someday come under attack.

October 8: Our country went to war yesterday in a far-away place. Selfishly hoping it all goes away. I must maintain the Peace Testimony right now most of all.

I was not going to church at this time, but I continued to embrace the Quaker faith. I do not believe that war is ever the answer to the world's problems, and I was distressed when our country began sending troops to Iraq.

THE WORLD STILL TURNS

In spite of national tragedy, the earth continued to rotate on its axis, the sun rose and the moon set. One afternoon I received some exciting news from my son.

October 9:   Jon called and I'm going to be a Gramma! Jon and Tiff are
pregnant and very happy. Life will really change now, for all of us!

November 18: Just watching the clouds, the road, the landscape. I am at peace,
settled and satisfied with the notion that just Being is good enough, the moment is
as it should be. I'm wondering if this is how most people ae most of the time? Is
this introspective trait a gift or a hindrance? Sometimes I think my heart will
break: thinking, remembering, missing, ruing the past. What would it be like
if…..And then I think of who I am now, that I am a collection of experiences. I
Am my past. The pain of yesterday means that today's joy can be more easily
recognized and absorbed.

2002

I had never been drawn to Iowa for its beauty. Oregon was lush and
green with mountains, lakes, rivers, and the Pacific Ocean.   Iowa
could be beautiful in the winter with enough freshly fallen snow;
however, some years we didn't get much snow and brown fields
scarred the landscape as I drove the 70 miles past farms and pastures
to Marshalltown.   In addition, there was a staid conservatism that
permeated social discourse.   In July 1999, Tim and I had taken a
walk through the Knoxville Racetrack grounds where we had seen a
sign that stated, "Entrance only for Board members and their
Wives".   Men were still very much in charge of things in Iowa.

March 23: Steve just asked me how I am. I told him I'm doing well emotionally
which is mostly true. I have developed a growing repulsion for Iowa. This is a
barren, man-made, stripped-of-beauty part of the country. A land of hog lots,
river/creek pollution, man-made lakes and waterways, a place of litter and
rudeness. A place of naïve prejudice, unhospitable to the outsider. It is a cold
place, a fabricated place where trees grow in a straight unnatural line, for they
have been planted by man. And I purposely use the masculine pronoun to
explain who has been responsible for this desecration. For this is a paternalistic
place where women are still the subordinated servants. This patriarchal society

has not kept step with the rest of the world, nor do they wish to do so.   It's almost as if Iowa is in a black hole, a no-where lost-in-time land where nothing changes, everything remains the same.

PART IV: THE JOURNALS

2002 - 2012

2002

THE NURSES

I met Dixie, Liz, Kathy, and Jane in 1983 in a study group at nursing school. In the Spring of 1984, we celebrated completion of our final nursing exam by staying at The Tolovana Inn at Cannon Beach. We meet every Spring or early Summer for a reunion and, as the years pass, we cherish our time together. We have gone to resorts, beaches, Las Vegas, Disney Land, the Grand Canyon, and we even went on a cruise. We represent different faiths (Episcopal, Catholic, Mormon, Agnostic, and Quaker), and we all specialized in different areas of nursing (Obstetrics, Geriatrics, Cardiology, Office Nursing, and Hospice).

We have weathered divorces, new marriages, deaths, (our parents and one child), childbirths, surgeries and numerous losses and trials. We take turns choosing where to go each year. In May, Dixie, the Mormon, had invited us to Salt Lake City for our weekend.

May 11: Weekend with the nurses last weekend at Salt Lake. Very meaningful, very bonding, and we all about cried at the end. We've all changed so much and our mortality seems so much closer at hand, thus making life more precious. We all seem so much more fragile this year somehow.

We have never missed a year and have now met for thirty-six years. There have been a handful of times when one of us couldn't make it and as we age some of us face physical obstacles and limitations for travel. However, our bond is unique and genuine, and we don't plan to give up our yearly gathering any time soon. We will be emotionally and physically (if possible) present for each other as long as we have breath.

NEW LIFE AND THEN DEATH

Lucy Jean, my first grandchild, was born on my father's birthday and I couldn't wait to see her!

May 19: I became a Grandma yesterday morning at 7:14 A.M. when Lucy Jean entered the world. Jon called me right away, within minutes, which meant a lot. He sounded so happy.

June 15: Oregon trip was great! Baby Lucy is a doll – so perfect! Jon and Tiff are getting worn down. Saw everyone. Mom not doing as poorly as I thought.

Kent's mother lived in Florida where he went to visit her for a few months each Summer. We knew she had lung cancer but didn't know how serious it was until Kent called Steve from Florida to tell him she was very ill and had been placed on a ventilator. Steve flew down to be with Kent and, in her dying breath she told Kent to "listen to your father".

June 23: Kent's mom died six days ago. So Kent is back home now. So hard to tell how he's doing.

I began crying at work one day in July and couldn't stop. I had stopped taking Zoloft in 1998 (after my overdose while in Salem) and had been experiencing disturbing "wreck" dreams at night and intrusive thoughts during the day. I sought advice from the facility psychiatrist and my colleague Doug Steenblock who called a fellow psychiatrist in town. I had an appointment with my new psychiatrist before the end of the day.

MOTHER

Mom was going to be 80 years old on August 17th and I arranged to have a birthday party for her in her home. Invitations were sent to family and friends who came from far and wide to wish her "happy birthday". Blair Sneddon, my cousin's husband, took Mom aside to discuss her living situation. He was concerned, as we all were, that she continued to live alone, and he feared for her safety. She had always had a soft spot in her heart for him, so he was surprised when she became angry with him. She forbade him to ever speak to her about it again.

August 24:   Went to Oregon for Mom's 80th birthday.   Good time.
Exhausting. So hard to part with my kids.

September 15: I am now taking Zoloft for depression. The outlook is less dim
now, the heaviness and darkness are abating some.

2003

February 27: Fred Rogers died today. As I watched him, heard him tell me he
liked me and that I was special, tears came to my eyes. I was not a child when I
first saw Mr. Rogers. Actually, I was on my Senior Skip Trip when I first saw
him. Why did I become tearful? I guess because his show, his presentation was
the last, pure, straightforward explanation of life. No sugar-coating, but no
cynicism. That will never happen in this society with such power, ever again.

I continued to call Mom almost every day. One evening the phone
call I had been dreading finally came: the Meals on Wheels man had
found Mom lying on the floor by her bed - she was now in the
hospital. I hopped on a plane and soon found myself in a conference
room at Stayton Hospital with my brother and his whole family.
Her doctor, Dr. Barnes, explained to us that she had most likely had
a vascular event, although she hadn't had a major Cardiovascular
Accident. She was deliriously happy and not at all aware of her
situation. She would never return home.

June 6: Mom had one too many TLA's and is in a skilled care facility. Still
impaired physically, cognitively, can't understand why she can't go home. She was
in Stayton Hospital for one week. I thought we had lost her at one point. Two
plane trips to Oregon. This has all taken its toll. Reestablished relationship with
my brother. I feel as if I'm hanging by my fingernails emotionally.

Larry and I made the difficult decision to place Mother in a skilled
rehabilitation facility. We had hoped that she would be able to
transfer from there to an assisted living facility in Salem. One day
Larry called after I had returned to Iowa and said, "I have good news
and bad news. The good news is that Mom's mind has cleared up

some and the bad news is that she's hopping mad". Her mind hadn't entirely cleared up, but just enough to recognize that she was no longer home. She became enraged when one of the men from her church told her that her car was no longer in her garage. (We later discovered that her license had been revoked but she had continued to drive around town). She called her grand-nephew Eric who was a newly licensed attorney and asked him to sue me. I am thankful that he did not follow through with her request; however, to this day I believe he has ill feelings towards me.

Her cognitive and physical status fluctuated over the next month. One day a nurse from the facility called to say that Mom was deteriorating and that I should come. I walked into the facility as a staff member was pushing her in a wheelchair down the hall. I didn't recognize Mom at first because she was so unkempt and small. She was shriveled up into a ball and she didn't recognize me either. Her face lit up as I greeted her, and we sat with her doctor in the facility lounge to discuss the next course of action. He asked her what she wanted, and she said, "I don't want to hurt anymore". He said "Jessymae, from this day forward you can eat, drink, get out of bed or stay in bed if you want. It's up to you." As I walked him to his car his shared with me that his own mother had died that very morning. I am so grateful for him being there for my mother that day.

She was placed on "Palliative Care" and I remained at her bedside for the next seven days. Beth had been visiting her frequently in my absence and now she began dropping by every day. Brother Larry began to visit as well. After our visit with her doctor she stopped eating and would only accept small sips of water. As Larry and I were visiting together at her bedside one day she opened up her eyes long enough to say, "It's worth it all to have you both together again". Otherwise she mostly slept. One evening, I worried that the head of her bed may be too elevated and asked, "Mom, do you want to lay down?" With her eyes still closed she replied, "It's LIE down".

Those were the last words she spoke. She died two days later. The last words my mother spoke were to correct my grammar.

November 7: Mother is dead. What can I say, what words to place in a succession to describe, no, explore the profoundness of that reality. Only in my dreams do I experience the anguish, and in those dreams the horror is that she is still alive in her befuddled demented state. I was with her when she died. Larry was also present. And I helped prepare her body, still lying on her bed, limp and soul-less. And I felt nothing.

She has been gone for five months, and still I feel numb. No tears. The house has been sold. If anything, a burden has been lifted. A burden of knowing how miserably depressed she was for thirteen years since Dad's death. A burden of frustration that she fought unrealistically and ridiculously to maintain her independence when her body would not allow her to do so in any dignified fashion. And then the horror that, in spite of her demands to never be in a nursing home, that is where she lived out her last days. If one can even perceive that as living.

She backed into death, fighting and kicking and scratching until her last breath as if, because of her uniqueness, the reality of death could never apply to her. She could not envision the world without her.

I feel some pain now and then. Glancing at the phone machine to check for messages and knowing that none of the messages will be a long rambling discourse from Mother reminds me that she is gone. But I did not like those messages, full of subtle suggestions of self-pity. I dreaded the weekly and then more frequent phone calls I felt obligated to make.

In fact, the last decade has been increasingly horrid as our relationship deteriorated into one of exasperation, pretending, anger, and resentment. The mother-daughter relationship crumbled until I was forced into the position of helpless overseer. All my knowledge of the aging process, depression, death and dying, the power of acceptance, was totally and absolutely useless. I was reduced to the helpless hand-wringing adult child of a stubborn demented parent.

I was the executor of Mother's estate. I met Larry about nine months after her death for lunch in Salem to give him a check for his part of the inheritance.   We visited and commiserated about the loss of our mother as we ate and I did not talk or speak to him for the following three years.

JIM

Steve's younger brother Jim still lived in his hometown of Oskaloosa and visited his mother every day for dinner.   We went to Thanksgiving at her home and Jim was not feeling well. Lumps in his back had been surgically removed, and a CAT scan revealed that he had lung cancer.   A few days later his workplace called his older brother Gary when he didn't show up for work and Gary found Jim still at home, lying dead on the floor.

December 7: Another death to grapple with: Steve's youngest brother Jim died.

December 1st. Cause of death? Lifestyle choices. The funeral parlor was packed with friends and family, and it was clear that he was dearly loved. He had a Bachelor of Arts Degree in Business Administration and had worked for the local lumberyard as bookkeeper since he graduated from college and had never married although he had several girlfriends through the years.

He spent evenings and weekends playing the bass guitar in bands, drinking, and using drugs; singing, playing, living as if there were really no reasons to take life seriously. So, I guess it is a blessing that, as he neared 50 years of age, he died, and that life stood still for him in the world of rock and roll. He died with a catsup bottle and two bottles of beer in his fridge. And he will be forever young as the rest of us continue to grow old.

2003 – 2008: THE QUIET YEARS

Life tumbled along with work, play, and trips to Oregon.   I sporadically attended the Friends Church in Oskaloosa, but it was thirty miles away and I felt intense loneliness when sitting all alone in a pew.   My emotional and mental health had somewhat plateaued as I continued to take an antidepressant and met with a therapist a few times each month.

December 26, 2003: I cannot say that I have inner peace. It is, rather, more of a simmering (beneath the surface) distorted jigsaw of gyrating shapes and forms, fighting for the priority position. In my heart I want to pick apart the past, to make some sense, some meaning of it all. Life has no meaning if I can't believe in some sort of order and positive direction. To not believe would mean existential crises. To not believe would suggest that we are here by accident and that pure hedonism is perfectly acceptable.

No, I cannot toss out the hope of a loving and caring God. I'm looking forward to some sort of moment of clarity, some flash of comprehension ("Oh, I get it now!"). Like in the future, at some point, all of the elements, past and present, of my life will gel together. And then I will know meaning.

Brendan James was born to Jonathan and Tiffany on July 7, 2004, exactly one year after the death of my mother. He was healthy, and his big sister Lucy was happy for him to join their family. I returned to Oregon several times after his birth. Beth was completing a teaching degree at Western Oregon State University while Nate was completing his Bachelor of Arts Degree in English. Both of my children and their families appeared to be managing well.

December 4, 2004: It's been almost a year since I last wrote. The year wasn't that bad, but self-reflection just seemed to be too painful. I continue to smoke, and I don't attend church. My new grandson Brendan is beautiful, and my granddaughter is a bundle of joy. My children seem to be happy and well. My job is, for the most part, fulfilling.

March 12, 2005: Looking back, its fairly transparent that my mood disorder has been a life-long struggle. Fortunately, the depression rarely takes a nose-dive but, rather, dips down into an angst-driven dysthymic existential cavern, never quite making it to the bottom. The free-fall began with my father's death in October 1990. His death initiated a series of life-altering disruptions, and my world, as I knew it at the time, began crumbling. After that, one rung after another began coming loose on the ladder of life. I almost fell off of the ladder completely, but somehow managed to hold on tight and kept climbing or at least kept myself from falling off.

June 26, 2006: I'm still alive. What I do is not who I am, but what I do affects how I feel about who I am: my self-image, self-esteem. I pray these days to God, that He/She will not give up on me. My mother's words echo in my ears: "Phyllis, you're a selfish selfish little girl". My life continues to be a charade. I cannot see into the future. I'm afraid to plan too far ahead because I can't see me anywhere in the future. I'm afraid I'll crash, descend into a frightening tailspin into psychosis, just lose myself to the black forces. The world is so scary now. Some say I'm strong for having survived and endured. They do not know I'm hanging in suspension by the flimsy thread of commitment and a teensy ray of hope. The times I have been truly happy and contented have been when I sincerely sought God's will and strove to be Christ-like. Forgive me Lord. Lead me in the way I should go. Grant me strength. Restore my faith.

A CHANCE MEETING

One cold February afternoon, I received a phone call from my mental health colleague Doug Steenblock. "Phyllis, Obama is here in the lobby. Get over here!" Barack Obama had declared his intention to run for president and was touring the Iowa Veterans Home. (Presidential candidates are known to frequent veteran facilities in Iowa where the first caucuses of the nation are infamously held.) I ran across the courtyard as snow clung to my sweater and as I stepped into the administration building I was greeted by the Commandant (the facility CEO). "Mr. Obama, I'd like you to meet our psychologist Doctor Martin".

 I was gob-smacked as Mr. Obama warmly shook my hand, placed his hand gently on my shoulder, and asked, "Doctor Martin, what do you perceive as the greatest needs for our veterans today?" I struggled to put some verbs and nouns together and replied that I was concerned about our troops returning from Afghanistan and Iraq with traumatic head injuries. A picture of the two of us walking together and talking in earnest sits on my bookshelf. The following

February I was in a crowded elementary school gymnasium in Des Moines caucusing for Barack Obama when my cell phone rang. Beth was calling from Fort Rock, Oregon and I answered "I'm sorry Honey. I can't talk right now. I'm at the Iowa Caucus." She replied "I know. I'm watching you on TV".

2007

A NEW JOB AND A MOVE

Depression waxed and waned over the years, but I kept putting one foot ahead of the other. I took antidepressants, and, at times, relied on antianxiety medication when fraught with nightmares and anxiety. My supervisor Mark had, over time, become moody and mercurial and had begun "micro-managing" my practice of psychology. Other staff members were occasionally the object of his wrath and criticism, but he seemed to be particularly focused on my performance.

I had been working with a patient with borderline personality disorder and together we had identified specific behavioral boundaries to help him reign in his impulsive behavior. One day this patient demanded to see me ten minutes before the end of the workday. As specified in his agreed-upon behavioral plan, I reminded him that this was inappropriate. I promised to see him the following day. This individual marched over to Mark's office and lodged a complaint. I was told by Mark the next day that I was being "put on probation" because I should always respond to a patient's request for therapy. That was the last straw.

March 25: I have decided to find other employment and it is such a relief! It is time. I wish I could work for Mark. I get so frustrated when his words strike me down, that I cannot self-talk myself into rationality, that when he "reprimands" me I am immobilized emotionally for several days and usually get back on me feet only after an extended period of time. Why does this happen? What dynamic within myself results in such pain? Whatever the case, I am leaving one way or another.

I called my old mentor Bob Hutzell at the Knoxville V.A. asked him if he knew of any job openings for psychologists at the V.A. He was happy I called because a new job opening had just been posted for a psychologist to be aligned with the V.A. Visiting Nurse Team. I was hired; however, I took a month-long vacation in Oregon before jumping into my new job as the psychologist on the V.A. Home Based Primary Care Team in the fall. Steve was being transferred to the Des Moines V.A. from the Knoxville V.A. and we bought a house in the Beaverdale neighborhood in Des Moines. We lived close to the hospital and took no time settling into our new life.

2008

BABY DANIEL

I had purchased plane tickets and had planned to be present for my daughter's first childbirth experience which was predicted to take place the third week of January, but Daniel had other plans. I was sitting in front of the fireplace one Sunday morning reading the Des Moines Register and sipping coffee when my phone rang. Beth said "Mom, I'm bleeding. Oh, I'm sorry I have to go. The doctor is calling!".

Beth had graduated with her teaching degree from Western Oregon State University the previous year and was teaching in Fort Rock, an extremely remote area of Central Oregon. The doctor told her to come to the hospital as soon as possible so Beth and Nate began the one-hour drive to the hospital in Bend while I secured a plane ticket and boarded a seven-hour flight to Redmond Oregon. It was snowing as I stepped off the plane and I was fortunate to find a taxi to drive me to the Bend Hospital from this tiny rural airport.

Beth had required a caesarean delivery. She was resting quietly in her hospital bed holding a little blanketed bundle when I finally entered her hospital room at 2:00 A.M. Beth and Nate had not been prepared for his birth and I remained for the next week assisting with housework, meals, and changing diapers.   Beth was eventually able to return to her students while Nate remained home during the day and worked at the restaurant across the street in the evenings.

2009

SMOOTH SAILING

February 2: Almost two years since last entry. Amazing events – Daniel Hays Fleming was born 1/7/08.

February 4:   I am working at the Des Moines V.A. and we moved to Beaverdale (love our house!). Beth and Nate moved to Glendale – much more secure with his family support and she gets to stay home with Daniel.   Jon and Tiff and kids moved to Austin Texas. GE moved them. Lucy is now six, Brendan is four. Sweet healthy kids. Wonderful visit in Oregon with Beth then Jon and family were here for Thanksgiving. Major back surgery on 12/31/08. Going to work today. Surgery was successful! I have made close friends at work. Oh yeah, Obama is president!

I had suffered with back pain my entire adult life and was pleased that the back surgery was successful. I adhered to a strict physical therapy regimen, and within four months I was back on the bike trails, biking 30-40 miles a day.

July 15: Life is so very good right now. So thankful.   All the facets, surfaces of my life are shining brighter. Life is amazingly calm, and I believe I am content. Content but still seeking. What do I offer today? Which gifts will I share? The gifts I've been given are not mine to keep. I am confident that I am in the midst of fulfilling my life mission to serve others. In giving, sharing, loving, I continue to grow.

WOUNDED WARRIORS

I was engaging in psychotherapy with World War II, Korean War and Vietnam War Veterans. They relayed details from grisly combat-related experiences: fires, explosions, blood, body parts, fear, panic, and paralyzing helplessness. One veteran described seeing soldiers trapped in a burning helicopter, screaming for mercy and asking to be shot to be put out of their misery. Another described how, at the age of 18, he was forced to kill small children when he was ambushed by them wielding machetes in the jungle. Many of the men expressed the heartbreak of watching their comrades fall in a rain of bullets, and I listened with compassion as sobbing soldiers poured out confessions of guilt and shame. I had become a member of the Hospice and Palliative Care Team along with my other responsibilities and, at times, often visited with veterans, while seated in a chair scooted up close to their beds.

July 17: I saw a 69-year-old veteran today who broke my heart. He was raised Catholic and he "hoped" he was going to Heaven. He was informed this morning that he probably has less than a few weeks to live, but he wants to make it to his birthday and have "chocolate cake and a beer". He turns 70 in six days. He was angry and afraid, and explained that he had done many horrible evil things to others. There was no way he wasn't going to escape the wrath of Hell for these deeds. He began to relate his traumatic Vietnam War experience: How he stabbed a Viet Cong in the back; that he sprayed Napalm under orders multiple times, knowing that it would kill all life in its way, that he also knew that other soldiers were killed in the process and his actions resulted in multiple deaths.

He had never spoken of these experiences to anyone and was adamant that he did not want to talk to a priest. He talked of carrying the weight of guilt since his return from Vietnam and said "I can't tell this to anyone. They don't understand. They can't understand." I told him he had already been to hell. He tearfully thanked me and said "please come back". I hope he's still alive on Monday.

His bed was empty when I returned to visit him the following Monday.

I learned about the "starts and stops" of life when I was five years old. I watched in horror as my dog Flicker ran out of the underbrush carrying a baby rabbit in his mouth. I hit him on the nose and screamed until he dropped the rabbit at my feet. The little creature was lying very still but I could see its chest rapidly moving up and down. I ran into the house with the bunny and Mother got a shoebox, lined it with Kleenex, and gently laid the bunny inside. She said something about needing to feed him milk, but we didn't have anything with which to feed him. She drove across town to the Sorg's home and borrowed a tiny doll bottle, returned home, and together we tried to get the bunny to suck on the bottle.

As a typical five-year old I got distracted and temporarily forgot about the medical crisis playing out in our kitchen. Later that day, Mother informed me that, in spite our efforts, the bunny had died. I looked at the lifeless form in the shoebox for some time, but it continued to just lay there, motionless. I remember well the sobering realization that a living breathing being had ceased to exist. Alive and then not alive. Not sleeping. Dead. Forever. Gone.

One afternoon, I was asked to see a dying veteran in the hospital. It was late on a Friday and the day had gotten away from me. As I hurried through the corridors to his unit, I wasn't too concerned about whether I would have enough time to visit with him. After all, he had less than one week to live and would probably be confused, weak, and unable to tolerate a very long session. As I approached his room, I realized that I was thinking more about whether I would be able to leave work on time than the fact that I was just about to be speaking with a human being about his imminent death. I was a bit chagrined, but still looked at my watch. Fifty minutes left in the day. Piece of cake.

I gingerly entered his room and saw an emaciated elderly male lying very still in a hospital bed, eyes closed with his oxygen tubing positioned awkwardly in his nose. Was he already dead? I greeted him formally as usual. "Hello Mr. Jones. I'm Dr. Martin. I'm a psychologist. Your physician asked me to come see you because she thought you were a bit down in the dumps."

He opened his eyes wide, looked at me, weakly smiled and said, "of course I'm down in the dumps! Who wouldn't be? She told me I only have about four days to live!"

The veteran warmly invited me to "pull up a chair" so I could sit close to him. "So what do you think about dying?", I asked him. "What do you think happens when you die?" This is not the usual opening topic of conversation for most people meeting for the first time, but we both knew why I was there. Why beat around the bush? The clock was ticking.

"I think that when I die that's it. No Heaven. No Hell. The end. On the other hand, how would we know? No one has ever come back from death to tell us". "How do you feel about that?" I asked.

"Oh, I suppose there might be something after life, but I don't believe in Heaven or Hell. Especially Hell." I thought of the old Blood Sweat and Tears lyrics "*I don't believe in Heaven but I pray there ain't no Hell*".

"I've had a good life", he said. Then he launched into a detailed description of how he had lived his eighty-five years on this earth. He related how he had been married for 43 years, how his wife had died, and how he had lived with multiple women since then "only one at a time". He told me how he had been raised as a devout Catholic, and that he had planned to be a priest until he realized how much he "loved the women". He told me about World War II and how he hid in the ditches and trenches in Germany, how he wore the same wool socks for six weeks until they fell apart, and how he would do it "all over again". He told me about his RV and his horse, his life as a long-haul truck driver, and about the time his boat took on water just as he was hauling in a huge trout on Lake Chelan in Washington State. He told me about how his first wife was his true love.

"Sounds like you've had a very full life. Very meaningful......."

(THERAPEUTIC SILENCE)

"So, you were raised in the Catholic Religion. Do you still believe in God or Someone like that?"

On we went about very deep stuff. Did he believe in anything or anyone beyond himself? It was important for him to process this. I had seen too many patients who, when confronted with mortality, began to wonder if the religious teachings of their early childhood may indeed be true. The reality of their unavoidable death can, in the last days, become a very terrifying notion. Especially terrifying if they believe, way down deep inside somewhere, that Sister MaryAnn was right: they may be going to the Hell that they've been trying so hard not to believe in during most of their adult lives.

"I've had a long life. A good life. And I knew this day would come. I don't like it, but that's the way it is. I've been very lucky. And I'm not afraid". I could see he was, indeed, at peace. And maybe our "psychotherapy session" had helped him come to grips with the "start and stop" of life. I thanked him for his time, he thanked me for my time, and we agreed to meet again on Monday, both us knowing full well that he could die before then.

I squeezed his hand, and, as I left, I said, "you know, you may want to think about that Heaven thing. You may be in for a wonderful surprise". He smiled, nodded his head, and closed his eyes. As I exited through the sliding doors of the hospital, I looked at my watch.

DEAR JONATHAN

September 12: Happy birthday Jon! Thirty-five years ago, my life was spontaneously changed when you came, very reluctantly I must say, into this world. I first learned about self-less giving because of you. I found that the whole of life was much larger than my narcissistic one-ness, and, as I gladly embraced the role of motherhood, I enveloped you as an extension of my being, yet you were uniquely separate as your own self. I am profoundly amazed at this richly complex, warm and generous man who is my son. How can it be that my infant-child, a genetic representation of myself, would become this amazingly intelligent, creative, self-assured husband and father? How is it that I was chosen to be your mother?

Through the years we have both changed and grown. We are now in separate worlds and our daily focus is on the immediacy of our surroundings. But a psychic, almost physical connection is ever-present, just barely under the surface of awareness. For you will always be my son, an extension of my existence, my legacy. Words cannot begin to describe the depth of emotions, the breathless mother-love, the breadth of pride in my heart. When you were born, my only prayer was that you would become a loving, caring person. That's all I wanted. I didn't care what degrees you would earn or how much money you would make, or whether you would be able to support me in my old age. My only desire was for you to be loving and caring.

My prayers were answered, and, I believe those core values helped determine the direction of your life. You have chosen your paths wisely, and for that I am also proud. My love for you is well beyond the limitations of the English Language: Maternal love extends beyond description or comprehension. It is part physical, spiritual, and psychic, a bond that will exist throughout all time. Life is a continuum. One day begets the next, one generation spawns another. We are but a small thread in this tapestry. As the leaves change, we will continue to grow and evolve. Who knows where or who we will be tomorrow? But whatever happens, whatever the seasons bring, you can depend on the reality of my never-ending love for you.

2010

LIFE GOES ON

January 4: With all good intentions I bought a "Complete Idiots Guide: Buddhism". We'll see.

January 7: In order to achieve "enlightenment", "self-actualization" or whatever it is that drives one toward contentment, one must learn to be transparently honest with herself.

January 17: I feel as if I am finally in a progressive state of restoration.

January 20: I am thinking that, in many ways, these are some of the best times in my life. Never have I been so content to be myself.

January 30: I had a moment of panic today while walking toward my government car after seeing a patient. I suddenly realized that this very healthy and happy period of my life could come crashing down at any time.

February 1:   *This day is a new day – freshly fallen snow*
So pristine, glistening, smooth and
In mounds.
Higher here, lower there, irregular shapes…
What unknowns lie beneath the snow?
As time passes all will be revealed.
But today I'll wear my best boots with
Strong soles.

My love for Steve remained strong and our relationship was comfortable and fun. I began attending Grace Methodist Church and I joined a group of women ("The Girls") who met once a month just to have fun. After reviewing research and scholarly papers about Substance Abuse, I made the decision to drink wine now and then with my new friends. I realized that I had never really been an alcoholic because my symptoms were never consistent with diagnostic criteria for a "Substance Related Disorder" (Diagnostic Statistical Manual-5). When I entered both treatment centers, everything I did and said was interpreted through the lens of assumption and bias that I was there because I was a raging addict and/or alcoholic. "When all you have is a hammer all you see a nail". I am, however, thankful for the spiritual guidance gained in Alcoholics Anonymous and am grateful for the support I received there during my darkest years.

April 4: I still catch my breath when I accidently see Steve at work or when I look out the window and see him working outside, or even when I look up to see him intently perusing a car magazine. I continue to be amazed at his ability to recognize and analyze such a variety of topics. His knowledge base is amazing. And I appreciate his humility so much! I just want Steve to love me enough to allow me to be true to myself, to continue to grow into who I was created to be.

April 5: The notion of religion without guilt is impossible to comprehend. I am jealous of others raised in less condemning faiths.

June 6: I think I'm working too hard at this "life" thing.

I found opportunities to provide training and in-services to medical staff at the V.A., and once again, I   received invitations to speak at a variety of conferences, primarily in the topic of Mental Health, Hospice/Palliative Care and Decision-making Capacity as it relates to Dementia. I was honored in June to give a presentation at a national V.A. conference at Johns Hopkins University on the diagnosis of Delirium.

June 13: I gave a presentation in Baltimore last week at Johns Hopkins and it was very well-received. I feel I must write my memoirs. I do have a lot to say and think my words may be helpful to others. Plus, I need to leave a legacy for my babies, to send them forward with wisdom.

October 16: Lots of dreams. A repeat dream about an attic – no - a huge upstairs in a very old house – full of treasures. Others know that the upper rooms are over-flowing with precious antiques, heirlooms, history, but no one has time or interest in even climbing the stairs to see what may be there. Some of the "others" include Ron and his family but there are faceless "others" as well. So, I have treasures in my mind – in the deep recesses that must be tapped before I die.

Memories from the wreck were never far away, and I was especially prone to intrusive memories during the Fall. A leaf blown across the windshield, a pedestrian stepping prematurely into the crosswalk, even the sweet smell of Fall were sensory reminders of that pivotal moment in time.

November 8: I will not write that today a little girl died. I cannot speak of the twenty-year-old pain or of the butchering of my soul. I must not give words to the stolen joy and dare not describe how the serrated knife of remembering continues to decimate the whole.

Jon and family visited for Thanksgiving and Steve and I flew out to Portland to celebrate Christmas with the kids. I had begun visiting Oregon three to four times a year and was developing a close bond with my grandchildren.

2011

A NEW POSITION

I was approached about moving to a new position at the V.A. position which would give me opportunities to consult with medical staff and provide ongoing education and training. I loved to teach and believed it would be a perfect fit. I would be helping patients with behavioral changes necessary for improved health, facilitating groups, consulting with medical staff and teaching. However, I would no longer be doing psychotherapy.

January 3: "Time, time, time…what has become of me?" (Simon & Garfunkle)

Seize the day but don't have a seizure. Okay, it looks as if I'm starting the year with a bit of an edge.

January 21: My new position at the V.A. is exciting! It is as if all that I have done, learned, lived, has been combined and that all that I am has blended into an almost perfect knowledge base and skill set.

March 10:   Walking carefully at times but maybe not today.
The life I live….
Sensing the abyss which echoes from below
The low-hanging wires above
Knowing

This suspension bridge I trod upon hangs from
A few threads.

March 13: Time just rolls on like ocean waves. Some days it seems that there is no movement, too still, too stagnant. And some days the tsunami crashes down hard, then sucks everything out and then in and I lose my foothold and fall prone in the sand. On the best days I ride the not-too-large waves gracefully and land softly at the end of the day.

STEVE'S CORVETTE

Steve traded in his 1968 Satellite Convertible for a 2002 red and black Corvette convertible. We had joined a Corvette club and he was obsessed with washing it, waxing it, and driving his new toy.

March 23: *Don't wait for me in your Blood Red Glistening*

    Topless World.

    Caress her Body Soft Touch Fragrant Oils

    Van Morrison and Mose Allison on Surround Sound

    Gentle firm hand

    Fondling fingers careful cautious

    Largo – adagio -allegro

    She moans, groans,

    Crescendo – screaming

    Screeching Tires.

ILLNESS

In April I began vomiting uncontrollably and, after a few weeks of doctor appointments and temporary remedies, I was admitted to the hospital where I remained for one week. I had been receiving cortisone shots for my back and hip and was taking four Aleve tablets each day. After several intrusive diagnostic procedures, I was finally diagnosed with an "abnormality in the bile duct". I was advised to never receive cortisone shots or take Aleve, Ibuprofen or Aspirin again.

October 30: How long does it take to grow up?

November 4: Had another birthday. This last year has been, overall, fairly crappy with a few high points. My health has been poor with chronic hip pain and GI issues. I can't have another year like this last one. So I will now shake the shackles of self-pity, remorse, and resentment. Had one of those existential "Is this all there is?" moments this afternoon. Not a good place for this girl to be.

THE CHRISTMAS BLUES

My entire family was planning to come to our home for Christmas and I had been making plans for the past year. Meals and outings were scheduled, and the refrigerator overflowed with food. Christmas cookies, cereal mix, banana nut bread, and cinnamon rolls were prepared, and I waited with great anticipation as the date drew close for our Christmas celebration.

December 11: Beth and family arrive in one week, then Jon and family come in eleven days. The forward concern is how I will manage after they're gone. On December 26th how do I get up and just move forward if everything I've been focusing on has been the past?

We had a magical meaningful visit. We all went ice skating (well I watched), to the movies, to a basketball game, and the little ones squealed with delight as we drove slowly past Christmas lights. We stayed up late, ate too much and laughed until we cried. I had never felt so close to my family.

December 30: I began to crumble emotionally on 12/26. By the time they were gone the next day I was literally in itty bitty pieces of despair and hopelessness. It is not listed in the DSM, but I had what can best be described as a nervous breakdown. Steve drove me to my nurse practitioner (I couldn't see to drive through the tears) who started me on Valium. It's an awful black place. This mostly relates to my desperate need to move back to Oregon. I need to be closer to my family, my people, my home. Steve is extremely supportive. He is loving, kind, understanding. My soulmate.

2012

January 25: I rise, dreading the day ahead. If I'm lucky, I drive alone and buy a latte and muffin at the coffee shop – a nice treat. I park, wait for the shuttle, then open up my unlit office. One by one I turn on the lights, methodically. My office is as neat as a pin. I look to see if I have phone messages. I turn on the computer. Any job postings? No. And then I know the day will be long, very long. I'm so efficient. I keep all of my affairs tied up in a neat bow of orderliness. I have purged my office of all that would be unnecessary or superfluous in Oregon. I could have my office packed in fifteen minutes. The day shuffles along. Patients, documenting, groups, meetings. But there's empty time, space to fill. Go to the bathroom. The gift-shop. The canteen. Take a walk outside. Move the hands of the clock along. Until its time to pack my purse, straighten my desk, put on my coat, and turn off the lights. I walk to my car and then go home to an empty house. An empty evening ahead. And so here I sit, writing in front of the fire. Late. The morning will come too soon, and the sameness will resume once again.

March 14: Went to psychiatrist in Ames. He is knowledgeable, warm, and patient-centered. He said "Phyllis, you're severely depressed but we can fix this!" How hopeful.

April 20:   *The Becoming of Old*
           I have become without knowing.
           Rambling along, paying notice, on occasion

To a grey hair, a stiff knee until one day
I look down and see my mother's hands.
No jewelry can hide the crevices, the irregular spots
And wrinkles
And when I wear her ring, I feel so close to her.

April 30: I want to cry. So, I go on as if....as if I feel no pain. So, I become who others expect me to be...someone in no pain. A woman of depth and humor. But it's hard acting, especially when the audience doesn't know you are even on the stage.

May 8: Dear Mother God. Grant me the grace for today. Remind me to be patient, to love others, to be selfless.

IMPULSIVE DECISIONS

I went to Oregon for a short visit and impulsively stopped by the Roseburg V.A. which was about a 30-minute drive from Beth's home. It seemed to be divine intervention when I was spontaneously offered to interview for the same job I held at the Des Moines V.A. I assumed that it must be providence, that God was smiling on me.

May 12: I got the job at Roseburg VA!

May 28: They still come – the episodes. They still come – the dark clouds. Dark and ominous, agitating. Will the tears fall, or does it just look like rain?

Beth was going to have another baby, and I bought plane tickets dated for a few days before her due date. But once again, this baby decided to come early. On July 7th, the same date as his older cousin Brendan's birthday and the ninth anniversary of my mother's death, Zachary was born by an emergency C-section. I arrived one day after his birth and stayed for a week in their home in Glendale. Jonathan and his family moved back from Austin to Portland a week later.

July 22: Beth had a blessed little baby Zachary on July 7. A C-section and I couldn't get there till the next day.

August 23: Tomorrow is my last day at the Des Moines V.A. Then driving across the country.

CRAPPY JOB

We packed up Steve's pickup and my Volvo and headed across the country to Roseburg Oregon where I had already found a small apartment. Steve returned to Des Moines and planned to retire in December. He was going to sell our house and join me in January.

This new job was not what I was expecting. I was not able to work with any patients, but instead was instructed to spend most of my time "consulting" with medical staff. My direct supervisor was a physician and I was a member of the medical team rather than the mental health team. The reception I received from staff was cold and unwelcoming because my supervisor had told them that I was coming to "tell them how to do their jobs". My position of Behavior Health Coordinator stemmed from the recognition that many medical problems relate to a patient's "noncompliance" with their treatment plan. V.A.'s all over the country were hiring psychologists to assist doctors and other medical staff motivate their patients to engage in healthier behavior and I was supposed to help them "motivate" the veteran with the goal of improving their health.

I had provided "Motivational Interviewing" training to the Des Moines V.A. medical staff; however, this medical staff was resistive to change and wanted nothing of it. My job also required me to drive to outlying clinics in distant rural areas where I had to stay overnight. I was alone every night, had no companionship, and my days were lonely and long. I began to question whether I could remain in this job. I spoke with the director of the Mental Health department at the Roseburg V.A. and was told a new psychology position might open, but that it wouldn't be any time soon.

December 15: Work is....trying. Still not enough to do. I'm hoping a regular Mental Health job comes up. And I've been quite lonely.

2012

I went to a new psychiatrist in Roseburg who prescribed new medications to help adjust my mood. I do not recall exactly what I was taking, but I began to feel emotionally blunted and mentally foggy. I tried to visit Beth and Jon as much as possible and they began to worry about me and questioned the wisdom of my decision to move to Roseburg.

February 3: It has been a very dark winter. Emotionally so much that I don't even want to write about it. My job really is emotionally difficult. I hate it. Trying hard to be positive. Very hard.

One day my supervisor sat down with me and told me he was not happy with my performance. I wasn't surprised. The job description was vague, and his expectations had been unrealistic. This was not at all the same position I had held at the Des Moines V.A., although I had the same title as "Behavior Health Coordinator". I decided to resign, and I called up my old supervisor in Des Moines who said that my previous position there had not yet been filled. She told me I could step back into my prior duties as soon as I could get there.

Steve flew out and I left most of my belongings with Beth and Goodwill Industries. My little Volvo was packed tight as we rolled back to Des Moines. Our house in Des Moines had been on the market but at the last minute the house sale "fell through". Steve unpacked the house and things were soon back to "normal". My stay in Roseburg felt like a dream because nothing had really changed in Des Moines.

PART V: THE JOURNALS

2012 - 2020

2012

BACK TO DES MOINES

When I returned to the Des Moines V.A. I saw Dr. Bahls, a neurologist and the Chief of Staff, in the hallway at the V.A. We had served on several committees together and he knew me fairly well. He pulled me aside and asked me if I had Parkinson's Disease. I realized then that I needed to discontinue taking all those psychiatric medications with their nasty side effects, so I returned to my former psychiatrist who prescribed a different course of treatment. Within a few weeks I was back to "normal".

April 7: Back in Des Moines. Grim year. Mentally trying to break out of this anxiety-ridden prison.

Much had changed during my brief absence, and some of my previous job duties had been taken over by two new psychologists assigned to the medical clinic. My opportunities for patient contact were limited and I spent more time facilitating weight loss classes, smoking cessation groups, and teaching classes. I was a member of the pain management team, but my obligations there were limited to intake assessments and psychometric evaluations. I tried to be innovative and resourceful and, for the most part remained busy. But I missed doing psychotherapy.

I joined Grace United Methodist Church, exercised, began knitting, and developed a close relationship with Teresa, the Director of the V.A. Homeless Domiciliary. She and her fiancé were members of the Corvette club where we shared several mutual friends. Teresa and I also enjoyed spending time with "The Girls" and provided mutual support for one another throughout the ensuing years.

2013

June 7: I hate work. What a mess I made moving to Oregon! It feels like a very bad dream. So surreal. I can't believe I was ever there. And now I'm back but I came back to a kettle of fish. Mother was right: There's one thing worse than having too much to do. It's not having enough to do. It's as if Mother is punishing me for how the end of her life turned out. Should I have quit my job and moved back? Should I have dropped everything to come back and care for her? I'll never know.

STEVE'S WRECK

I received a call from Steve's cellphone one afternoon while I was at work. He had gone on a bike ride in Oskaloosa and I assumed that he was calling to let me know when he would return home. A strange woman's voice asked me if I was "Mrs. Halverson" (I hadn't changed my name and I knew something was wrong). She was a nurse who happened to be out on the bike trail when she came upon Steve who was lying on the trail next to his bike. She explained that he didn't know where he had parked his pickup and he was confused. Should she call an ambulance? Duh. I called my supervisor and sped down the 45 miles to the Oskaloosa Hospital Emergency Room. Steve recognized me, but he appeared to be in a daze. I was terrified that he may have a head injury. He was transferred to a hospital in Des Moines where he underwent a ten-hour surgery to repair his pelvis and hand. He was even more confused and delirious after surgery, and I envisioned growing old with a cognitively impaired husband. The doctor finally ascertained that he was experiencing a negative response to Dilaudid, a powerful pain medication, and within twelve hours he was back to his usual self.

July 15: Steve had a bad bike accident. Crushed his pelvis and broke his hand. Now I'm home caring for him. I'd certainly rather be here than at work!

November 28: Work has improved. I had my annual evaluation and got an "excellent" which means I get a bonus. And things have picked up. Some.

MILLIE

Steve's 97-year-old mother Millie was a tiny but sturdy soul, the granddaughter of Norwegian immigrants. She still lived alone in her own home. Her oldest son Gary and his wife Janet lived two houses away and they assisted her as needed. One Saturday, we decided to visit her and stopped at a Subway to buy her favorite sandwich. She met us at the door with her walker, tiny and folded over because of kyphosis. We sat with her in the living room munching on our sandwiches. Steve asked, "how are you feeling these days Mom? She smiled and said, "oh I'm fine!", and she continued to visit with us about church, family, and friends. The next morning Gary called to let us know that when he had gone over to her house to get her for church, he had found her dead, lying on the floor by her bed.

December 28: Steve's mom died on December 15th, the day after we visited her. Steve is fairly non-plussed and I don't think it's hit him. But maybe. She was so frail and, at 97 years of age, it wasn't a surprise.

2014

April 5: It's amazing! I can actually say I had a good work week! I moved into a new office and that has really raised my spirits. Plus, things are going better at work.

May 3: Had a great trip to Oregon! Saw the kids, friends, nurses, even "ran into" Larry at the airport.

I had been at the Denver Airport waiting to board the plane when I saw my brother. We were on the same flight and we visited for about twenty minutes as we waited to board. We were civil and polite and hugged one another "goodbye", but it would be a few years before I saw him again.

August 22: Dr. Trahan (my psychiatrist) put me on Lithium. He thinks I have "Unipolar Depression".

September 28: I have stepped out of the darkness. Steve retires on Friday.

December 25: My faith is growing, or maybe healing. Attended the Christmas

Eve Service last night with Steve. I couldn't sing all the songs because I would start crying.

2015

January 1: The ache of depression is whispering to me, beckoning me to fall as I have in the past. Ten months until retirement. I'm fearful that something is going to happen before then. But today I'm okay.

January 4: I've been contemplating how to navigate the year ahead. I've left the door ajar, allowing myself to believe in a loving God who orders our ways. This is a bit scary. Trusting God. I haven't really done that since 1991.

I had begun my life as a psychologist with the intention to never retire. I loved helping people and, at first, every facet of my job had been exhilarating and rewarding; however, my final psychology position had become boring and I fiercely regretted leaving the Home-Based Primary Care Team. There were no other psychology positions available within the Des Moines V.A., and I was stuck in an unfulfilling job. I was sad to being exiting my job with a whimper instead of a "bang".

RETIRED

May 16: Official retirement date has been set for August 31st. Counting the weeks until then.

September 1: I'm retired. Wow.

Steve and I took off for a one-month vacation to Oregon two days after I retired. We stayed at a beach cabin overlooking the bay in Netarts and I knitted and read while he took long walks on the beach. The kids joined us for a few days, and it was a refreshing start to this new chapter of my life.

Election commercials and ads begin very early in Iowa because it is the first state in the country to caucus for presidential candidates. Donald Trump had been making frequent appearances around the state and I was appalled that someone with his depraved character could ever be considered worthy to run for president.

September 24: Troubled by Trump, Mexican Immigrants, refugees. Can't believe so many people endorse Trump. He's a very bad man. And then the injustices towards the immigrants. As a country our response has been horribly selfish. And then there are refugees in Europe. How horrible for them! And I must ask myself: What am I doing about it?

The kids came to our home for Christmas and we had a lovely time. I was not distressed when they left because I was now retired and knew that I was free to visit them as much as I desired. Steve and I had been discussing the notion of moving to Oregon since I retired, and we began to make tentative plans to move.

2016:

April 27: Geraldene (my cousin) died last week. Prince died. Hillary is winning. I am so troubled by Trump, even more because of the number of bigoted followers. He is actually winning on the Republican side. Who are these people? I am afraid of them. I am afraid of White Republican Christians.

In July, our entire family attended a family reunion in Halfway, Oregon, the birthplace of my parents. Nate had been moody, grouchy, and withdrawn during the entire trip, and I wasn't surprised when Beth called a few days after we returned to report that, after seventeen years of marriage, they were splitting up. Nate drank an excessive amount of alcohol, had lost a great deal of weight and I suspect that he may have been using methamphetamines. Beth worked for a nonprofit organization in Salem and was excelling professionally, while Nate stayed at home as a "house husband". She would come home from work to find dirty dishes, a messy house, and piles of laundry. He was gone most nights at the local theatre doing stand-up comedy for which he received no pay.

July 30: Beth and Nate are getting a divorce. For the first time in ages I am missing my mom. I just want to talk with her. But I am relieved that Beth is going to be free of him.

Hillary Clinton was the Democratic candidate for president, and I joined other Democrats making phone calls, knocking at doors and attending campaign events. I was excited about the prospect of having a female president, but more importantly, I was desperate to keep Donald Trump from winning the presidency.

October 11: Emotionally stable. I flew in my dreams, which is good.

POLITICAL ANGST

November 20: I went to bed on November 8th hoping for the best and fearing the worst. I was staying with an old college friend Gail Ragsdale in Oregon and the past few days had been quite pleasant as we visited about the past. However, I knew that her husband was a right-wing Republican and I had begun to suspect that she was not as passionate or interested in the upcoming election as I was. When I awoke on November 9th, I checked my phone. My son had sent me a one-word text: MOM!!! I quickly perused my phone and realized that my worst fears had come to pass.

I called my like-minded progressive activist husband and as I cried, we consoled one another and encouraged each other to just try to get through the day. I dressed and tearfully greeted my friend in the kitchen, fully expecting her to commiserate with me about this horrible thing that had come to pass. Instead, she said, "There really wasn't any real good choice this election" and "it'll be okay, there are checks and balances in place, so I am not concerned." I was heartbroken and could not verbalize a coherent retort. I mumbled something about needing to leave and headed for the home of Sheri, my old Mapleton classmate.

As I tearfully drove up the Interstate, I wondered about who was driving the other cars. Did they vote for Trump? Were they racists? Did they hate women? Were they delusional? Then I began to think about my Republican family and friends. Did they vote for Trump? They did. Fear and bewilderment washed over me. WAS I SAFE?

198

When I arrived at my friend Sheri's home, she ran to me, enveloped me in her arms, and we sobbed together. Her husband had been up since 4:00 a.m. weeping and raking leaves. I knew I was safe. I was with my people. I remembered that day in 1980 when I sat on the end of the bed with Jonathan and wept when Jimmy Carter lost the presidential election. Later that day Jonathan told me that Lucy, now 14 years old, had cried herself to sleep on election night because she knew that Hillary had lost the election.

December 4: I am brokenhearted, devastated. Trump won. On Lorazepam. Can't really talk about it.

December 31: I have been thinking a lot about moving to Oregon. It is about time. As Steve says, I've paid my dues.

2017

NEVERTHELESS SHE PERSISTED

I donned my pink "pussy" hat on January 21st and joined over 15,000 women in January as we marched around the perimeter of the Iowa State Capitol. I knitted almost 20 pink hats for friends and family and felt desperate to make my voice heard by the world. Bigotry and hate had no place in my country, and I worried about the divisiveness that was tearing apart our country. The Women's March was an exhilarating and inspiring event. I realized that although I was surrounded by strangers, I was not alone in my grief. We shouted slogans of solidarity, hope, and peace as we made our way around the capitol and I wondered if I could do anything to make even a tiny difference in this shaky world.

Steve and I discussed our responsibility to make a positive difference in our own corner of the world and we explored various ways to utilize our knowledge base and skill sets. Steve volunteered to be a Court Appointed Special Advocate (CASA) for foster children and I volunteered as a Long-Term Care Ombudsman, visiting nursing homes and advocating for resident rights. I also joined a local bipartisan organization and spent many evenings writing postcards and letters to elected officials to voice my concern about the wave of treacherous policy and legal changes occurring on the state and national level. In April I traveled to Oregon and was blessed to spend time with my old friend Sheri Mahaffey. She accompanied me to a tattoo parlor in Salem and held my hand while I had "NEVERTHELESS SHE PERSISTED" tattooed across my lower back.

HELPLESS

We had purchased a trailer, situated on a small lake in Northern Iowa, and spent our summers on the deck overlooking the water. My vertebrae had progressively deteriorated and I would never again be able to ride my bicycle, so I knitted and read while Steve took bike rides and hikes. One day I was sitting in the pickup in a parking lot at an ACE Hardware store in Spirit Lake, Iowa while Steve was getting supplies for the trailer. I heard a commotion and looked up to see a few men running alongside a car driving slowly on the highway. I thought at first that a dummy was being pushed underneath the car but in a split second realized that a woman was stuck under the front of the slowly moving car.

The woman under the car was waving her hands and screaming as I ran to join a few others who were shouting at the driver to stop when suddenly a pickup sped in front of the car and screeched to a stop sideways in front of the car, forcing it to stop. I rushed to the front of the car and knelt on the pavement with the woman who was still wedged under the front of the car. She was conscious, and I tried to comfort her as we waited for the ambulance. I could see blood oozing from under the car and thought, "she's going to die right here, right now, and there is nothing I can do to help". I felt faint as the ambulance pulled up. I stepped back to see Steve running towards me and sobbed as I fell into his arms. The driver was an 87 -year-old man who had just been to an ophthalmologist around the corner. He had run over this woman as he drove over the crosswalk and turned onto the highway. The next day, the evening news reported that the woman was in critical condition, but later I read in the Des Moines Register that she had recovered from her injuries.

I was, of course, traumatized by this experience, and when we returned to Des Moines, I resumed seeing my psychologist for counseling. I decided with my psychiatrist that the side effects of Lithium were too mentally and emotionally blunting and he prescribed a new antidepressant. I weaned myself off Lithium, began taking new medication, and felt increasingly alive and energetic within two weeks.

LIFE GOES ON

June 5: Steve and I are planning a move to Oregon next spring. Have been going through diaries. Have a plan for my book. I'm still very agitated about Trump. I just want to crawl into a cave to wait until this nightmare is over. I'm very proud of Beth. She is doing a great job as a single mom and is secure in her job with a three-year contract. I will be very happy to be closer in proximity so I can be more of a support. And Jon…what can I say? He's the perfect father, husband, and son. I'm so proud of them both!

August 7: I'm quite perturbed that Jane posted on Facebook that she is still "for Trump" and says that Larry supports him even more than she does. I have fantasized about just cutting them all (Larry and family) out of my life. I can't believe that anyone of even mediocre intelligence could still endorse that horrible man!

August 30: I am at an emotion impasse. As long as Trump is in office, I am going to experience a certain degree of anxiety and angst. His behaviors continue to be repulsive, appalling, and frightening.

November 27: Disturbing dream last night ended with a nondescript man moving my furniture out of my room as I protested. He stated "You're nothing more than a car wreck" then I awoke. Is that how I see myself subconsciously?

All that I am and all that I've accomplished only adds up to "a car wreck" when all is said and done?

December 12: Good news tonight! The Democratic challenger won over the creepy Moore character to land a Senate seat! This is so encouraging to the Resistance! I awake every morning hoping to hear that Trump has been ousted, resigned, or died.

2018

MY DYING REQUESTS

I was scheduled to have another extensive back surgery, and I had concerns about surviving the rigors of another surgical procedure. I decided I should clarify my last wishes.

January 3: I'm going to make sure I have left in place instructions about my care if I suffer cognitive impairment or die. First, someone please log onto Facebook and tell my friends.

1) *If I suffer cognitive impairment*
   a. *please take me to the pool so I can swim!*
   b. *Do NOT place me in a nursing home! Medical foster home okay.*
   c. *Make sure I have adequate pain control*
   d. *Do not talk to me like a kindergarten teacher. I am still Doctor Martin. Speak to me as such.*
   e. *Try to make me laugh.*
2) *If I die:*
   a. *Give Beth $30,000 or enough for a good down payment on a house*
   b. *Give Brendan and Lucy $15,000 each for their college fund.*
   c. *Keep my violin (keep it in the family), the small chest full of my diaries and journals (made by my Grandpa Sanders for Mom when she was three years old), And the picture of Mother with Great Grandma Schneider.*
   d. *Take my ashes to Halfway and bury them next to Aunt Elsie Martin*
   e. *Lucy, take my journals and write a book*

f. *Lucy and Brendan, stay optimistic but angry enough to change the world for the better. Resist ignorance, hate, and bigotry. Look to your wise parents and Auntie Beth for guidance.*

g. *Beth, you can do this. Stay strong. Find friends to laugh with and cry when you need to.*

h. *Jon, it's okay to lean on others sometimes. Keep laughing often. Do what you love.*

i. *Steve, do not isolate and hibernate. Remarry. Take a risk and trust others, even strangers. Find what makes you laugh and do it. Try Yoga or meditation. I want so much for you to find peace!*

j. *Daniel and Zach, love each other deeply and never forget to love and have compassion for others. And treat your mother like the most important woman in your life, like the queen that she is.*

k. *Tiffany, what a joy you are! You do not need to be everything to everybody, but you need to know that you are the strong steady hand that holds this family together.*

l. *If you decide to write an obituary, use the graduation picture where I'm tossing my head back and laughing.*

m. *If Larry comes to my funeral don't let him sit with family.*

PRAYER

February 27: The world, politics, people are so fucked up right now. Another school shooting on 2/14 but this time the kids are stepping up. Therein lies our hope. My generation can only do so much.

March 8: Prayer: How can I pray for God to provide us the "perfect" house in Oregon when dead two-year-old immigrants are washing up on the seashore in Europe? How can I ask that my family be kept safe when so many people are dying of starvation and so many are fleeing their war-torn homes? So much agony, pain, and unrest in the world! School children being gunned down, so many minorities unjustly detained and killed, thousands of prisoners, mostly minorities, receiving subpar care and unjustly jailed. How can I possibly make such a selfish request of God? But then I remember how, when I was ten years old, I prayed for a sign that Mother was safe and hadn't been hit by a train and, magically the record player started skipping. Someone answered that simple child's prayer. So, I know there is a Someone who hears and acts on prayer.

BACK TO OREGON

Steve and Kent took a long bike ride a month before we moved to Oregon.   Kent was 33 years old, had completed his Associates Degree in Graphic Arts, and was dating Andrea, a spunky articulate young woman he met on a dating app.   He was determined to never marry or have children and Steve suggested to him that he may want to reconsider this stance.   We were both proud of Kent who had grown to be a responsible and conscientious adult and were happy when Kent and Andrea invited us over to dinner to announce that they were engaged to be married.

May 14: We loaded all our belongings into a moving van on April 26th and headed out to Oregon in the pickup. We arrived in Oregon April 30th.

We purchased a modest three-bedroom home in Stayton, Oregon and began to settle in.   Steve and I   began painting, sanding, scrubbing, weeding, and worked together to make this house our home. Steve became a CASA for the state of Oregon, and I was pleased to find a community swimming pool close to our home. Our home was close to Beth and only about a one-hour drive from Jonathan's home in Portland.   We began to forge closer bonds with my grandchildren, and I obtained my Oregon license to practice psychology with hopes of eventually being able to volunteer.

Jane (my brother's wife) reached out to me, and we began going out for lunch on occasion.   Our visits were somewhat strained, but I still had the ghost of a desire to maintain contact with my brother's family.   I had lunch with one of my nephews on November 1st after some brief communication through Facebook, and he shared with me that Larry and Jane's relationship had been "just a financial arrangement" for decades.   He wasn't sure if his father even lived at home anymore.

2019

A LONG WINTER

I had resumed smoking when I retired and decided to finally quit smoking. My doctor and I had discussed my smoking history and he had prescribed Chantix (a medication to suppress nicotine receptors). I began to feel ill on November first and after about three weeks, my condition had not improved so I quit taking Chantix which has a potential side effect of gastrointestinal discomfort. However, after discontinuing the Chantix, the nausea and pain persisted. After inconclusive extensive (and expensive) diagnostic procedures, the Gastroenterologist in Portland finally suggested that my gastrointestinal system could no longer tolerate antidepressants.

February 9: I have now been ill for 3 ½ months with 26# weight loss. We did manage to do some fun things: We went to Florence for a weekend and had dinner with my cousins, attended a music festival, Paula and Jesse drove down and we went to the Women's March in Salem. I'm getting my grand piano back! (I had left it in Oregon with Ron who gave it to Jon and Tiffany who gave it to her sister Shannon in Portland).

February 28: I have really enjoyed having lunch with Beth or just popping in when I'm in town. I'm thinking that perhaps being back in my children's and grandchildren's lives may be why my emotional state continues to be fairly good.

I had lost 40 pounds by April and, for the first time in many years, I could not take an antidepressant. As my strength returned, I began attending the Silverton Friends Church and, on occasion, was privileged to play the piano for the Sunday worship service.

April 20: Tomorrow I'm playing piano for church and I'm thrilled! Steve has been attending church with me most of the time and I'm happy to be back among Friends.

MY THEOLOGY

May 8: My Theology:

- *There is no Hell after life. (I can't believe in a God who would eternally punish one of Her children); God is genderless. But since I was supposedly made in God's image, I use a feminine pronoun.*
- *Jesus was born and lived and probably rose again.*
- *Salvation is whatever a person needs it to be. We are saved by love and compassion. We are saved by our own acts of kindness.*
- *Heaven is a human construct. We cannot fathom the dimensions that exist beyond our time-limited, start and stop lives. We cannot grasp the notion of ETERNITY so we create places that fit neatly into our limited paradigms.*
- *The Bible contains much truth and wisdom. It is a spiritual guide. It is not THE word of God.*
- *The Bible was written by patriarchs and scholars as they strove to gain some understanding of Who is OUT THERE?;*
- *True freedom is found when my life is congruent with my morals and ethics.*

On August 31st We returned to Iowa for Kent and Andrea's wedding and Steve beamed as Kent and Andrea walked down the aisle to "I Found You" by Alabama Shakes. Steve had strived to be a good single father and often spoke of his concern that Kent would be "okay". After their wedding Steve told me that this had been one of the happiest days of his life.

READY TO CONFRONT MY DEMONS

I decided to poke around the internet to search for names of psychologists in the area. Although I was feeling emotionally stable, I knew that given enough time, (now that I couldn't take an antidepressant) depression would most likely rear its ugly head. I found a psychologist who was also a former classmate from graduate school, and I began seeing him weekly for psychotherapy. I resonated with his treatment approach and was hopeful that, over time, he would help me extinguish the demons from my past.

October 14: I found a new psychologist and it's a great fit! Nick was one year behind me in graduate school and earned his Psy.D. in 2001. I am hopeful that with psychotherapy and exercise, my mental health will continue to be good.

November 9: Yesterday Kristine would have been 36 years old. Beth was 13, Jon was 17, and Ron and I were 39 years old when I had the wreck. So, it's been 28 years. And this year, for some reason, is hard. So much anger and grief. Still.

> *A broken windshield*
> *A falling leaf*
> *A news-bulletin*
> *A child's shoe in the street.*
> *I notice. It all.*
> *I notice. Every day.*

BACK TO WORK

During my search on the Psychology Today website I recognized the name of another psychologist as a former colleague from my days as a visiting psychologist at the V.A. I contacted her to say "hello" and found that she had resigned from the V.A. and had started a business in the Salem area. She was looking for a psychologist to provide in-home psychotherapy.

November 13: I prayed, and I think maybe my prayer was answered. That puts me in an awkward position with God or Somebody or Jesus. I may be employed as a psychologist in the near future!

December 10: Jane is very ill, in ICU. Larry is being an asshole regarding updates.

Larry called to say that Jane was quite ill and was in the hospital. I offered to assist if needed but was told that she was only allowed to be visited by "immediate family". Jane was diagnosed with an autoimmune respiratory disorder and returned home where she continued to recover. I visited her as she reclined in a hospital bed in their living room. Larry was there masquerading as the dutiful husband, polite as usual. He gave me a stiff hug as I left, and I suppose that may be the last time I ever see him.

December 11: New psychiatric nurse practitioner, (Arvilla) good fit. She was a nurse at Woodstock! Some progress in therapy with Nick with whom I will eventually do EMDR (Eye Movement Desensitization and Reprocessing). Getting ready to go back into my chosen field.

Nick had administered a formal psychological assessment in November and shared with me that my profile was consistent with the diagnoses of Posttraumatic Stress Disorder (PTSD) and Major Depressive Disorder. He specialized in treating PTSD and I was looking forward to finally addressing some unresolved trauma.

2020

BAD THINGS HAPPEN TO GOOD PEOPLE

January 19: Eric Muhr spoke in church today about "Theodicy", the study of Christian suffering. I thought about the day I was told that God had allowed the wreck to happen and remembered that as a young adult I had read about Corrie Tin Boom who had been a prisoner at Auschwitz. She had written a book about forgiving those who have inflicted harm and proposed that "God doesn't give you too much to handle". First of all, I don't believe God makes bad things happen nor do I believe that God sits around thinking of ways to dump burdens on me or test my faith. I can't believe in such a fickle God. Bad things happen to good people. Period. But God is there to give me strength when I falter in the darkness under the weight of grief and pain, even when I forget She is there.

January 31: My psychologist Nick is in the hospital "critically ill". Great. Now he's going to die.

February 11: Well, he died of a stroke. That sucks.

I had sensed that Nick would die. I had seen him on the afternoon before his hospital admission and he had not been feeling well. He told me that he felt like he had the flu, but "not like any flu I've had before. He ached all over and said "the weirdest thing is that I have totally lost my sense of taste. I can't taste anything". I was concerned that he may be experiencing some sort of neurological event, curtailed my psychotherapy session, and advised him to seek medical care as soon as possible. The counseling office called to cancel my next scheduled appointment and told me that he was in ICU on a ventilator. I knew he was going to die.

February 22: The first draft of my book is written up through 1999. Writing about the wreck wasn't as hard as I thought it would be but reading and writing about those years with Rich was very difficult. Beth reminds me that I was in an abusive relationship and now, so many years later, I agree. I am reminded today to continue my search for truth, for this God who has never stopped caring, has never stopped loving. This God who, if I am open, will give me strength and grace for the day.

February 25: I am getting close to the end of the first version of my book. It has been an emotional journey and I wonder where and how my story will end.

EPILOGUE

When I was in college, Erickson's developmental theory stated that, as humans grow old, we naturally draw into ourselves and isolate from society. One popular example cited an Eskimo People who, when they recognized they were no longer of benefit to their community, would hop on an iceberg and float away.

My generation celebrated the first Earth Day on April 22, 1970 by picking up trash. We had dreams of peace and a free democracy; however, we got busy raising children, learning a trade or profession, and buying homes. Most of us didn't pay much attention to politics, but we had trust and confidence in the constitution and all that it stood for. While we were focusing on more immediate tasks, some members of our generation (even some with whom we had, at one time, shared a passion for justice and fairness) were busy amassing fortunes and funding self-serving policies.

It doesn't look like any of them plan to hop on an iceberg any time anytime soon. I also have no plans to fade away. I will continue participating in civil discourse, marches, and protests. I will vote. I will volunteer for campaigns. I may go to jail, who knows. But I will never set sail on an iceberg.

And so here we are. The presidential primaries are in full swing and I am hopeful that in November we will elect a president with some integrity. The Climate Crisis has bubbled to the top of public awareness as young people like Lucy and Brendan have risen up to demand action. The coronavirus has reared its ugly head and who knows where we'll be in a year from now. I am a member of the

Silverton Friends Church where I play piano on occasion, swim laps three to four times a week at the community pool, and belong to a local Book Club. Steve and I have made some wonderful new friends and are active in the local Democratic Party where I facilitate a group once a month ("Maintaining Mental Health in a Divisive Political Climate").

I am seeing patients in their homes, and I am once again realizing my childhood dream of becoming a safe reassuring presence to those in need. My love for Steve grows every day and we are happy to continue down the path towards the unknowns of tomorrow together. I take a medication for anxiety when needed and have tried to weave meditation and mindfulness sessions into my daily routine. God is ever present, and I will be able to swing with the winds of change as long as I have meaning and purpose.

February 27: I plunged into the pool today and I felt as if I was moving through warm honey. Thoughts, worries, concerns and responsibilities faded away as I began swimming the first lap. One stroke. Two laps. One stroke. Four laps. One stroke. Eight laps. Focus. Ten laps. One stroke. Fifteen laps.....One stroke at a time.

Beth continues to work for a robust non-profit foundation in Salem. She is managing magnificently as a single parent. Daniel and Zach appear to be healthy and content.

Jonathan owns a successful software company (Silverpine) in Portland.

Tiffany has chosen to remain at home helping Jon with the company finances until Brendan graduates from high school.

Lucy is an amazing young woman and plans to major in Political Sciences next year. She has been actively fighting for Climate Change legislation and has a passion for making a difference in the world.

Brendan is a strong sturdy redhead computer whiz who sold an "app" to Apple last year and spends time on the Willamette River with the Portland Rowing Club.

Ron works part time at United Way in Salem and plans to retire soon. He and Linda still live on the farm in Scotts Mills.

Nate quit drinking over two years ago, has a stable job, and is a good father to Daniel and Zach.

Kent and Andrea live in Des Moines where she owns a succulent shop and Kent works for a beverage distribution company. They do not plan to have any children. We'll see.

Larry is "retired" but teaches full time in the business school at Oregon State University.

Jane continues to heal.

TRUTH

She knew she could never find the answer in the four walls of the
place for Seekers,
for Seeking she had done there and sometimes the answer had come,
but now the questions were too deep,
burrowed into her marrow so that the thought of finding the answer
within those white walls seemed incredulous and stupidly naïve.
The answer would come, she knew, but not there.
Life had become too richly patterned, too full of deeply sliced
crevices
and the colors were wonderfully different, colors without names,
and forms with dimensions beyond reality.
The answer would come from a source yet unknown to her.
As a Seeker she knew it would come -as it had with the other Seekers
when they gathered to search for the answer.
But this time would take more – an intense yet passive effort.
This required patience and plodding, for the answer would be
revealed slowly, as life was lived
one step at a time, one breath, one joy, one heartbreak at a time.
The Giver of the answer had not forgotten.
Each day her eyes, ears, her very senses were being sharpened,
becoming progressively acute.
Truth was slowly appearing,
as the sun rose, as the fetus grew in the womb, as the fruit ripened
so the truth would be, as it always had been.
And someday, not in the Sepulcher
but in that new place, that new dimension
she would see that Truth had been within her
surrounding her…..
It was her essence all along.

BENEDICTION

God is not angry with you....

May you grow to love and accept the you, God is making you to be

May you walk in a new level of grace and gratitude, that gives you peace and leave others encouraged.

May you be more apt to look forward with hope than you are to look back with regret.

May your heart spill over with the very thought of the story God is writing in your life.

As you go along, always remember to do unto others as you would have them do unto you.

Amen. (Ron Woodward, former pastor of Silverton Friends Church)

You make beautiful things out of us.
You make beautiful things out of the dust.

ACKNOWLEDGEMENTS

I would like to thank my husband Steve for his profound patience and support as I have sought to achieve my long-stated goal of writing this book. I would also like to thank Teri Orahood for her expert editing, assistance, and encouragement throughout the composition process. Finally, I am immensely grateful to Max Marbles for patiently guiding me through the steps necessary for publication.

Phyllis Martin was born in Oregon in 1952. She received an ADN from Portland Community College in 1984 and was a Home Health and Hospice Nurse for twelve years. She received her BA in 1989 and was awarded a Doctorate of Psychology degree from George Fox University in 2000. She provided treatment for veterans in Iowa until 2018 and then returned to Oregon to retire. She returned to work as an in-home psychotherapist in 2020. Dear Lucy is her first book.

Made in USA - North Chelmsford, MA
1106289_9780989839297
05.14.2020 0914